SOUTH AMERICAN
FOOD & COOKING

SOUTH AMERICAN FOOD & COOKING

Ingredients, techniques and signature recipes from the undiscovered
traditional cuisines of Brazil, Argentina, Uruguay, Paraguay, Chile, Peru,
Bolivia, Ecuador, Mexico, Colombia and Venezuela

**Jenni Fleetwood
& Marina Filippelli**

southwater

This edition is published by Southwater

Southwater is an imprint of Anness Publishing Ltd
Hermes House, 88–89 Blackfriars Road, London SE1 8HA
tel. 020 7401 2077; fax 020 7633 9499
www.southwaterbooks.com; info@anness.com

UK agent: The Manning Partnership Ltd
6 The Old Dairy,
Melcombe Road, Bath BA2 3LR;
tel. 01225 478444; fax 01225 478440; sales@manning-partnership.co.uk

UK distributor: Grantham Book Services Ltd
Isaac Newton Way,
Alma Park Industrial Estate,
Grantham, Lincs NG31 9SD; tel. 01476 541080;
fax 01476 541061; orders@gbs.tbs-ltd.co.uk

North American agent/distributor: National Book Network
4501 Forbes Boulevard, Suite 200, Lanham, MD 20706; tel. 301 459 3366;
fax 301 429 5746; www.nbnbooks.com

Australian agent/distributor: Pan Macmillan Australia, Level 18, St Martins
Tower, 31 Market St, Sydney, NSW 2000; tel. 1300 135 113;
fax 1300 135 103; customer.service@macmillan.com.au

New Zealand agent/distributor: David Bateman Ltd, 30 Tarndale Grove,
Off Bush Road, Albany, Auckland; tel. (09) 415 7664; fax (09) 415 8892

A CIP catalogue record for this book is available from the British Library.
Previously published as part of a larger volume, *The Food & Cooking of the Caribbean, Central & South America*

Front cover shows carbonada criolla p114–5

Publisher: Joanna Lorenz
Editorial Director: Judith Simons
Editor: Clare Gooden
Assistant Editor: Lindsay Kaubi
Photographer: Nicki Dowey, Will Heap and Patrick McLeavey
Home Economists: Fergal Connelly, Joanne Craig, Tonia George and Lucy McKelvie

Stylist: Helen Trent
Designer: Nigel Partridge
Cover Design: Balley Design Associates
Additional Recipes: Rosamund Grant, Elisabeth Lambert Ortiz, Maggie
Mayhew, Kate Whiteman
Production Controller: Claire Rae

1 3 5 7 9 10 8 6 4 2

NOTES
Bracketed terms are intended for American readers.

For all recipes, quantities are given in both metric and imperial measures and, where appropriate, measures are also given in standard cups and
spoons. Follow one set; they are not interchangeable.

Standard spoon and cup measures are level. 1 tsp = 5ml, 1 tbsp = 15ml, 1 cup = 250ml/8fl oz

Australian standard tablespoons are 20ml. Australian readers should use 3 tsp in place of 1 tbsp for measuring small quantities of gelatine, flour, salt, etc.

Medium (US large) eggs are used unless otherwise stated.

ACKNOWLEDGEMENTS

Jenni Fleetwood would like to pay tribute to Elisabeth Lambert Ortiz,
Elisabeth Luard and Judy Bastyra, experts on the food and drink of Latin
America and the Caribbean, whose books have been an inspiration for
many years. In addition, she would like to thank Jane Raphaely for
sending her to South America in the first place, and the 107ers for
decades of support.

Marina Filippelli would like to thank her friends and family who were
always present with suggestions, advice and a healthy appetite. This book
would still be in the making were it not for Lizzie's help and Nick's infinite
patience and encouragement. Special mention also goes to her parents
who instilled in her a love for the food and culture of Brazil.

Additional picture material provided by South American Pictures: pages 7–21.

CONTENTS

A BRIEF HISTORY

South and Central America is a vast area comprising a large number of individual countries, each with diverse ways of preparing and serving food. The only thing they have in common is that they have all been subject to a Spanish or Portuguese influence.

The events that led to the domination of the continent by two European powers began when Christopher Columbus petitioned for support for a voyage of discovery across the Atlantic in search of a sea route to India. At first he was turned down, but King Ferdinand and Queen Isabella of Spain eventually agreed to his request, largely out of a desire to find a new source for the spices the people of southern Spain had learned to love when under the control of the recently expelled Moors.

Columbus set sail on 3 August 1492, and in October of that year he reached

Watling Island in the Caribbean. Convinced he had reached the Indies, he continued to Cuba and Hispaniola (now Haiti and the Dominican Republic). In 1500 the Portuguese explorer Pedro Cabral landed on the coast of Brazil, and two years later Columbus reached the South American mainland. The early explorers were not interested in conquest, but individuals such as Hernán Cortés and Francisco Pizarro were dedicated to it. During the 16th century they invaded Mexico and Peru respectively, while other parts of South and Central America fell to other conquistadors. In the process, great civilizations were overthrown and the stage was set for the total take-over of the continent by Spain and Portugal.

It was Napoleon III, the 19th century French emperor, who coined the term "Latin America" and applied it to those

Above: Introduced to the rest of the world by Columbus, chillies originated in the South American jungle.

countries on the American continent where Spanish and Portuguese were spoken, including the Spanish-speaking Caribbean islands and Mexico. The term is now used to include all the islands.

The term "Latin America" suggests that nothing of value existed before the conquest, and it does not acknowledge the indigenous peoples nor the great civilizations – Maya, Aztec and Inca – they spawned. However, the term has value, if only as shorthand, in giving some indication as to the major cultural and culinary influences in this part of the world in the post-Columbian era.

NEW SETTLERS

When the first conquistadors landed in Latin America, they had few cooks with them, and so local people were hired to prepare food, in this way they were introduced to dishes prepared with foreign ingredients such as corn, chillies, beans, squash, tomatoes and chocolate, the Spaniard's became particularly fond of chillies, chocolate and vanilla. The most important of these new ingredients was corn, which the indigenous peoples

Left: Although the cuisines of Latin America differ from country to country, there are some common ingredients.

called *maïs*. Like wheat, corn could be used to make bread, but it was more versatile. The husks could be used as wrappers; the stalks for training beans; and the silks as ties. The cobs could be eaten fresh or stored for the winter.

Where corn and beans grew, so did squash. This remarkable food also kept well and yielded delicious seeds. Tomatoes were another important find, as were chillies. When Columbus first tasted a dish made using these fiery red and green pods, he assumed its heat came from black pepper and named the pods peppers.

The ships that brought the invaders sailed back to Spain laden with produce, then returned to Latin America with settlers who brought their own bounty – cattle, pigs, sheep, wheat, sugar cane and nuts. Until this time some areas of South and Central America had few sources of meat.

Priests came to Latin America too. Their aim was to convert the native population, but they also had valuable horticultural skills to pass on. The South American wine-making industries were started by priests who needed a ready supply of communion wine.

Lands were settled and crops were planted, but such activities required labour. At first the native population willingly gave their assistance, but soon rebelled. The situation grew worse with

the *encomienda* system, which gave Spanish individuals land rights. The indigenous peoples were forced to work for no payment other than Spanish lessons and religious instruction. They were shockingly exploited and the work was hard, especially for those already weakened by disease. They died in their thousands from exhaustion and disease.

SLAVES AND SETTLERS

The colonists responded by importing African slaves to work the burgeoning sugar plantations. The Africans made a huge contribution to the regional cuisines, especially in Brazil. The climate was similar to their homeland, so the many vegetables and fruits they brought with them flourished.

The Spanish and Portuguese settlers intermarried freely with indigenous and African women and, as a result, the *mestizo* ("mixed") population grew.

The food became *mestizo* too. Many of the cooks were either indigenous or African women, and they prepared a mixture of their own recipes plus the dishes their employers wanted. Spanish

Left: Native South American ingredients are sold daily at a busy traditional vegetable market in Peru.

Above: The lost Inca city of Machu Picchu in the Andes Mountains is now a very popular destination for tourists.

ingredients – such as onions, garlic and rice – were incorporated, and Spanish dishes were adapted to include chillies, tomatoes and even cocoa. This two-way trade led to a vibrant Latino cuisine,

Other nations made a valuable contribution too. Indentured labourers from India, South-east Asia and the Far East have all contributed their own styles of cooking.

Latin America is a turbulent part of the globe where the only certain thing is change; this is as true of the cuisine as anything else. Immigrants continue to introduce new dishes, and tourists take away memories of delicious meals they hope to recreate at home. This time the trade is between Latin America and the world. While pizza becomes commonplace in Brazil, ceviche is enjoyed in Canada, and Californian chefs hanker for *huitlacoche* (corn truffles).

Latin America still has secrets to divulge. In the jungles and hidden Andean valleys there are undoubtedly new ingredients waiting to be discovered. These will add another layer to a cuisine that is as exciting as it is extraordinary.

BRAZIL

Whether it is because it is the largest country in South America or has such rich cultural and racial diversity, Brazil is a place that celebrates excess. The Brazilian people love to eat, love to drink and love to dance. A trip to this, the only Portuguese-speaking country in South America, is a glorious assault on all of the senses, and never more so than during Carnival, when the streets throb with the sounds of samba music and the vibrant colours of the costumes fizz like the fireworks that explode overhead. The food is just as exciting, Sample delicious seafood in Rio de Janeiro, unusual pork dishes in Minas Gerais, tender beef in Rio Grande or the

Below: The Amazon river and rainforest cover much of Brazil and are home to many unusual species and crops.

spicy specialities of Bahia, where Africa meets South America in an explosion of unusual and fiery spices.

EARLY HISTORY

Some 50,000 years ago primitive peoples crossed from Asia to America by way of the Bering Strait land bridge and began the long trek south. Nobody knows for certain quite when they reached South America, but hunter-gatherers were certainly enjoying the fruits of the Amazon basin by 8000BC. Fish, manatees, turtles, game animals and birds were plentiful, and they supplemented their diet with cassava (*manioc*), nuts and fruits that grew in the area. Some migrated to the coast, and survived mainly on shellfish, as is evident from the huge shell mounds that they left behind.

Above: Coffee berries are picked by hand when ripe, then exported around the globe in huge quantities.

Brazil did not have the great civilizations that evolved in Central America and the west of the continent. Instead, as the indigenous people abandoned their nomadic lifestyle for farming, settled communities or chiefdoms were established. As well as cassava, corn, sweet potatoes and squash were grown, often on the shell mounds left by their predecessors. The existence of these early settlers was not as peaceful as it sounds, however. At least one of the tribes, the Tupinambá, were cannibals who not only ate their enemies, but fattened them up first.

PEDRO CABRAL

In 1500, the Portuguese explorer, Pedro Cabral, claimed Brazil for Portugal, but he only stayed long enough to erect a cross, say a few prayers and take on board his ship some unusual wood that yielded a red dye – *pao Brasil*. His compatriots at home were not very excited about this new territory, but Portuguese merchants considered that the wood might be worth exploiting, and a few expeditions were mounted to cut down the trees. Trading stations were gradually set up along the coast to the north and south of Salvador de Bahia, and the country came to be known by the same name as the wood, Brazil.

In the beginning, these Portuguese settlers and the indigenous peoples co-existed amicably enough, but when what had been a minor timber operation began to escalate into a mass export operation, the natives began to withdraw their labour. They were even less enthusiastic about working on the many sugar plantations that had been established from the middle of the 16th century onwards. The Portuguese settlers tried to force the native South Americans by enslaving them, but so many died from exhaustion or disease that the plantation owners began to import African slaves instead.

SUGAR AND THE SLAVE TRADE

By the time slavery was finally abolished in Brazil towards the end of the 19th century, around four million African slaves had made the terrible journey from their native land to Brazil. Many did not even survive the long crossing, and many others died shortly after their arrival on the plantations (*engenhos*) where sugar was grown and processed.

A few successfully escaped to form their own secret communities, known as *quilombos*, while others survived their bondage by focusing on keeping alive their music, culture and religion, and cooking food similar to that which they enjoyed at home. It was the Africans who originally introduced ingredients such as black-eyed beans (peas), okra and yams to Latin America, and these

Dendê oil
African slaves transported to Brazil initially missed one of their favourite ingredients, dendê oil, which comes from the fruit of the African oil palm and is valued for its rich orange-red colour. Fortunately, they soon discovered that a similar colour could be obtained by adding crushed annatto (achiote) seeds to ordinary oil. Dendê oil is now widely used in Brazilian cooking, especially in Bahia, where the African influence is strongest.

thrived in a climate that was quite similar to that of West Africa. Food was used for purposes of ritual as well as sustenance, and some of the recipes cooked throughout Brazil today evolved from the foods prepared by African priestesses to offer to their gods.

GOLD RUSH

In the late 17th century, Brazilian explorers, known as *bandeirantes*, began to find gold in the mountain streams to the north of Rio de Janeiro. The ensuing gold rush led to a boom time in Brazil. Despite the relative inaccessibility of the main goldfields, new towns quickly began to spring up in the area that would later come to be known as Minas Gerais (which translates as "general mines").

Prospectors travelled to this area from all over Europe, hoping to make their fortune. Many of the country's sugar-cane planters also joined the gold rush, taking their slaves with them.

Above: In more cosmopolitan cities such as Rio, every imaginable cuisine from around the world is available.

Several years later, around 1720, diamonds were also discovered in the region, and for about a century, Brazil became the world's major supplier of both gold and diamonds. To this day, Minas Gerais remains one of the richest areas in the country.

THE ROYAL COURT

In 1808, after the occupation of Portugal by the French, the Portuguese royal court decamped to Rio de Janeiro, making the city the new capital of their empire. When King Dom João VI finally returned to Spain in 1821, he left his son Dom Pedro I behind to rule Brazil. Dom Pedro I was subsequently recalled to Portugal, but he defied his father and the Portuguese government and declared Brazil's independence in 1822, with himself as Emperor.

GERMAN FARMERS

Dom Pedro's wife, Empress Dona Leopoldina, conceived the idea of peopling the vast area of southern Brazil with European farmers to work the land. Thousands of German colonists arrived and settled in the state of Rio Grande do Sul. In places such as Novo Hamburgo and Blumenau, their culinary contribution is evident and remains today, with sauerkraut, sausages, spätzle and delicious sweet pastries.

COFFEE – THE NEW CROP

In the century following independence, coffee replaced sugar as Brazil's premier export product. Further foreign immigration was encouraged for the purpose of having enough labour to work on the coffee plantations. Immigrants, especially Italians, quickly followed by Japanese, Spanish and Portuguese, flocked to cities such as Sao Paulo. Coffee was the major source of income for Brazil in the 1870s and the 1880s, and in 1889 the powerful coffee producers helped to bring about a military coup after which Brazil became a republic.

Below: Large freshwater catfish are displayed for sale at the busy Ver o Peso market in the Amazon.

FOOD AND DRINK

There is a wide variety of food on offer throughout Brazil. In the coastal belt, where the majority of the population lives, cosmopolitan cities such as Rio de Janeiro, Salvador and Sao Paulo have every type of restaurant imaginable to choose from, including those that specialize in regional cuisine.

Among the specialities is *feijoada completa*, not so much a dish as a lavish feast. A huge platter of fresh and smoked meats, including pig's tongue, is flanked by black beans, rice, spring greens, farofa (flavoured toasted cassava flour), orange slices and several sauces, all washed down with *caipirinha*, which is a mixture of *cachaça*, sugar and lime. Although they have a burgeoning wine industry in the temperate south, Brazilians prefer to drink iced beer or *cachaça*, which is often mixed with fruit juice or milk.

Rice is grown in Brazil and is the most widely used accompaniment, along with the ubiquitous farofa. In coastal areas, fine seafood is on offer.

REGIONAL CUISINES

There are four main regional cuisines in Brazil, plus the cooking of the Amazon region, where roasted game, exotic freshwater fish and unusual fruits can be encountered.

Above: The traditional Brazilian Saturday lunch is feijoada completa, *a meal of meats, rice, beans, greens and farofa.*

Comida Mineira is the cuisine of Minas Gerais. For over a century Minas Gerais was the wealthiest part of Brazil, and it is still rich in minerals. Farming is also important there. Crops include corn, beans, coffee and fruit, and there are large herds of beef and dairy cattle. Pork is the favourite meat, especially *lombo*, pork fillet or tenderloin. Bean dishes are also typical of the region, a favourite being *tutu*, which consists of black beans cooked with cubes of bacon and cassava flour and served with meat. Minas Gerais is also well known for its cheeses.

The well-travelled chilli

When African slaves introduced the malagueta chilli to Brazil, few people realized it was a returning immigrant. It originated in Central America, was taken to the northern hemisphere by the Spanish and eventually found its way to West Africa, finally returning to the continent of its birth in the baggage of slaves bound for Brazil.

Comida Baiana is perhaps the best known style of cooking in Brazil, celebrating that province's connection with Africa. Popular ingredients here include okra, dendê oil, dried shrimp, coriander (cilantro), coconut milk and lots of fresh seafood. A popular snack is *acarajés*, tasty bean patties or fritters, split and filled with various sauces. *Moqueca* is an aromatic dish of seafood, tomatoes, (bell) peppers, fresh coriander (cilantro) and dendê oil, invariably served with farofa to soak up the delicious coconut sauce. Brazilians like to finish a meal with fresh fruit. Desserts tend to be very sweet and are often based on custards in the Portuguese style. Avocado is often served as a mousse or ice cream.

Comida do Sertão is the cuisine of the vast plateau in the north-east of Brazil and can be sampled in the country's capital, the purpose-built city of Brasília. Dried salted meat – *carne seca* – comes from this region and beans are used in hearty meat dishes. Pumpkins, peppers and corn also feature, along with exotic fruits such as guavas, mangoes and carambolas. Favourite sweetmeats of the region include candied orange peel and candied figs.

Below: A Bahiana street vendor prepares local delicacies for passers-by, including acarajés, *delicious fried bean fritters.*

Comida Gaúcha means meat and plenty of it. This describes the cooking style of the vast Brazilian cattle country down south. A big feature of this area are the popular *churrascarias* – restaurants where you can sample almost every cut of meat imaginable, including all types of offal and a wide variety of delicious sausages.

Above: Brazil is renowned for its spectacular Mardi Gras carnival, when everyone takes to the streets to party.

STREET FOOD AND SNACKS

Brazilians like to be able to eat wherever and whenever the whim takes them, so street food is always on offer. This ranges from simple hot dogs, hamburgers and toasted cheese sandwiches to the filled bean or cheese patties known as *acarajés*. Pastries on offer include *pastels, esfihas* and *empadinhas*, which are baby empanadas stuffed with a variety of delectable fillings, such as fresh palm hearts in a tasty savoury sauce.

FEASTS AND FESTIVALS

The main celebration of the year throughout Brazil is *Carnaval*. Rio de Janeiro is the city usually associated with this extravaganza, but Brazilians often prefer to celebrate by taking part in the less touristy but equally electric spectacles in cities such as Salvador, Recife and Olinda. The build-up to *Carnaval* begins soon after Christmas and reaches its peak as Lent begins.

ARGENTINA, URUGUAY AND PARAGUAY

The cuisines of these three countries have one major ingredient in common – beef. Argentines eat a great deal of it and Uruguayans eat even more. It is less popular in Paraguay, but even there you will often find barbecues piled high with tender steaks, ribs and parts of animals that you never knew existed. Few ethnic dishes survive in these countries, except in Paraguay, where the indigenous Guaraní once lived. Their traditional crops – cassava, corn and sweet potatoes – are still staples.

EARLY HISTORY

Although this part of South America was claimed by Spain in the early part of the 16th century, there was no rush to colonize the territory. The first of the explorers to come ashore, Juan Días de Solís, was attacked by hostile natives and – according to some records – eaten. This was a powerful deterrent, although it did not prevent one of the survivors of the expedition from pressing on to Paraguay and then Bolivia. Here he acquired some silver, which was discovered after his death on

Below: Gauchos on an Argentine cattle ranch demonstrate their riding skills for Dia de la Tradicion.

the return journey. This sparked a rumour that Spain's recent acquisition might hold riches. The country was christened Argentina, meaning "place of silver", but when reality failed to match rumour the Spanish lost interest. In any event, by 1531 they were preoccupied with Peru, where gold and silver was being "liberated" from the Inca Empire by Francisco Pizarro.

The first permanent settlements in Argentina were in the Andean valleys close to the border. Santiago del Estero, Tucumán and Córdoba were established in 1535. A year later, Pedro de Mendoza set up camp close to the Rio de la Plata, on a site that would one day become Buenos Aires. His hopes of founding a city were dashed, however, when natives attacked and he was forced to decamp to Uruguay.

Until the arrival of the Spanish, this part of South America was peopled by various tribes of hunter-gatherers turned farmers, growing crops such as corn, cassava, sweet potatoes, beans and peppers. Coastal peoples supplemented their diet with food from the sea – fish, shellfish and even seals. There were no great civilizations in this area, like those that existed in Peru or Central America. Pottery, stone carvings

Above: The different varieties of corn display many striking colours – here they have been left to dry in the sun.

and rock paintings survive, but few of the inhabitants themselves withstood the arrival of the Europeans. War and disease quickly decimated their numbers, and by the end of the 19th century, very few of the early people remained.

THE PAMPAS

In 1581 the Spanish made a second attempt to establish a settlement on the banks of the Rio de la Plata in Argentina, and this time they succeeded. The extensive plains, or pampas, surrounding the place they called Buenos Aires proved to be incredibly fertile, and agriculture was rapidly established.

Cattle and horses that had escaped the original settlement had bred freely, and vast herds of animals now roamed across the pampas. This unexpected bounty was exploited by gauchos, or cowboys, who broke the horses and corralled the cattle. At first the animals were mainly killed for their hides, but when large salting plants were established in the early 19th century, the beef industry burgeoned. The pampas were fenced off and huge estates, *estancias*, were quickly established. Only the very rich could afford to buy these estates and soon the landed class became the most powerful people in Argentina.

In 1816 the country, for the first time, became independent. During the second half of the 19th century, demand for cheap food in Europe led to further expansion of the beef industry and immigrants poured in. Meat processing factories, including the famous Fray Bentos plant just across the river in Uruguay, were built. At the same time sheep farming was becoming established in Patagonia and by the early part of the 20th century, Argentina was a major exporter of beef and lamb, wheat and wool. These remain important today, although now much of the pampas is given over to grain and oil seed farming.

AN ARGENTINE ASADO

The traditional way of cooking meat in Argentina is *al asador* – on the spit. The meat is impaled on metal rods, which are stuck into the ground at an angle to prevent the meat juices from dripping on to the fire. Whole carcasses or sections of carcasses are cooked this way, and the meat is sliced off and served after guests have enjoyed the traditional appetizers – kidneys, morcilla and chorizo sausages, livers and *chinchulin* (loops of stuffed intestine).

Below: The herbal tea drink, yerba maté, *is drunk throughout Argentina, and is often served in a dried, decorated gourd.*

FOOD AND DRINK

With so much good quality beef at their disposal, it is not surprising that meals revolve mainly around meat, which is usually served with a piquant sauce, *chimichurri*. Fish is not as popular as meat, despite being in plentiful supply, and vegetables are not much in evidence either. Meat consumption is lower in Paraguay, which, along with northern Argentina, is the only area where ethnic cuisine is still widely served. Corn meal is used to make delicious spoonbreads and puddings. Cassava, which Paraguayans call *mandioca*, is baked with cheese and eggs or transformed into flat breads that resemble tortillas. The influence of indigenous cooks is also evident in Argentine dishes such as *carbonada criolla*, a stew served in a pumpkin; and *humitas*, a puréed corn mixture which is often steamed in corn husks.

Immigrants have exerted considerable influence on the food of Argentina and Uruguay. The pasta and pizzas in Buenos Aires and Montevideo are as good as any in Italy, and the Italians also inspired an Argentine dish in which pork is baked in milk. The Spanish influence remains strong, but Middle Eastern, Chinese, Japanese and Korean settlers have also made their mark.

Above: In Buenos Aires, Argentina, a chef prepares large pieces of meat to be grilled at a traditional asado.

In the beautiful Lake District, where the Andes provide a towering backdrop to towns that look more European than South American, visitors can sample delicious fondues, sweet pastries or the local chocolate.

Yerba maté, a type of herbal tea, is the drink of choice in Argentina, Uruguay and Paraguay, along with wine, beer and *caña,* a cane spirit.

STREET FOOD AND SNACKS

Empanadas with various fillings are popular, as are tiny cheese and ham sandwiches. Pastries are often very sweet, especially the ones that incorporate *dulce de leche* (caramelized milk). Churros, the Spanish answer to doughnuts, are enjoyed with hot drinks.

FEASTS AND FESTIVALS

The most interesting festivals in this area are those that focus on the gaucho tradition. These include demonstrations of riding skills and the opportunity to sample a traditional *asado*. In Montevideo, the summer *Carnaval* is famous for the African drumming that accompanies *candombe* dance troupes.

PERU, BOLIVIA AND ECUADOR

Many of the world's most popular foods come from the arable Andean highlands of Peru, Bolivia and Ecuador. Potatoes originated in this region, as did tomatoes, squashes, pine nuts, quinoa, tamarillos, sweet potatoes and several types of bean. All of these foods were cultivated by some of the most fascinating civilizations the world has ever seen.

EARLY HISTORY

Unlike Brazil and Argentina, where no major civilizations were based, this part of South America has been home to a succession of highly developed cultures. Among these were the Nasca of Southern Peru, who etched the soil with elaborate geoglyphs so large that their shapes – patterns, birds and animals – can only be fully appreciated from the air. In the north of the country, the Mochica people built impressive pyramids, while the Tiahuanuco established an empire that ruled Peru, Bolivia, Chile and Argentina for over 1,000 years. Shortly after their collapse towards the end of

Below: Corn grows in abundance on the Incan agricultural terraces in the Peruvian highlands.

the 12th century, a Quechua tribe, one of many in the mountains, began to establish a power base in the area around Cuzco. Their leader, known as the Inca, was Manco Capac. Within 300 years the Inca empire stretched from Colombia to northern Chile and ruled over more than 15 million subjects. Aside from their military might, skilled governance and prodigious building skills, the Incas also improved farming by introducing terracing and irrigation, cultivating new crops such as cassava and peanuts, and elevating the already high status of corn by declaring that only the Supreme Inca himself could plant the first seed of the new season.

The Inca civilization endured until 1533, when Cuzco fell to the Spanish conquistador, Francisco Pizarro. Along with Ecuador and Bolivia, Peru (which at that time included the northern part of present-day Chile) became part of the Viceroyalty of Peru, administered first from Lima and then from Quito. A period of Spanish colonial rule followed, coming to an end when Peru declared its independence in 1821. Ecuador did the same thing a year later, and Bolivia followed in 1825.

FOOD AND DRINK

Their shared history, first as part of the great Inca empire and later under Spain, means that the countries of Peru, Ecuador and Bolivia share similar cuisines, though each country has its own specialities. The Spanish influence is most noticeable on the coast, while in the high Andes, Quechua people fought to preserve their customs, eschewing Spanish ingredients and cooking methods. Away from the big cities it is still possible to come across dishes that have changed little for centuries.

Potatoes are eaten extensively throughout this region. Cooks are fortunate in having a wide variety of potatoes to choose from, and they take great care in selecting the right type for the dish. The yellow Papa Amarilla, for instance, tastes great in *causa*, a Peruvian speciality, which has an infinite number of variations. One way of preparing it is to layer cooked potatoes with flaked fish, chopped tomatoes and avocado; another variation tops the potato with an onion sauce before garnishing it with hard-boiled eggs, lettuce, peppers and olives. Equally delicious is *ocopa arequipena*, in which cooked potatoes are covered in a spicy cheese and walnut sauce.

A typical Peruvian dish is *carapulcra*. Dried potatoes, a throwback to Inca days when potatoes were freeze-dried on top of the high mountains, then squeezed dry and placed in the sun until hard, are traditionally used for this dish, although fresh potatoes can be substituted if the dried variety are unavailable. Potato and cheese rissoles are extremely popular in Ecuador, while in Bolivia potatoes are often simply mashed with a little oil and lemon juice, then served with chopped cassava, locally known as *yuca*, and corn, both of which are staple foods.

One of the most fascinating Peruvian ingredients is quinoa, known as the "mother grain" by the Incas. The tiny grains have a mild, slightly bitter taste and firm texture, and should be cooked in the same way as rice. Quinoa is an excellent source of protein and can be added to stews, bakes or salads.

Above: At an Ecuadorian market in Otavalo, women in traditional costume buy fresh fruit and vegetables.

FISH AND MEAT

Bolivia is one of only two landlocked countries in Latin America. As a result, the inhabitants do not eat as much sea fish as their neighbours, but fresh fish in the form of trout from Lake Titicaca is very popular. Peruvians enjoy a wide variety of fish and are especially fond of corvina or striped bass. They also have access to excellent seafood. The Pacific seaboard is noted for its delicious ceviche, the dish famous for "cooking" the fish by marinating it in fresh citrus juices. Lime juice is usually used in ceviche but in Ecuador the juice of bitter oranges is preferred.

Although Peruvians produce beef and pork and enjoy both, they are particularly partial to duck and chicken and also like to eat *cuyes* (guinea pigs). These vegetarian animals are raised in much the same way as rabbits or hens, and smallholders will often let them range freely around their homes. *Cuyes* are also raised commercially, on farms. Popular ways of cooking *cuyes* include stewing in a rich sauce and grilling over an open fire. Other exotic meats can be sampled in the jungles of Ecuador, where animals such as wild boar and monkey are often eaten.

Because mountain-bred animals are often tough, their meat is usually chopped into very small pieces, then stewed with corn and the rocoto or mirasol chillies that are widely used in this part of Latin America. This helps to tenderize the meat.

Many fruits are grown in this region, including pineapples, cherimoyas, mangoes, guavas and passion fruit. Bananas and plantains are also widely cultivated, especially in Ecuador. Other important ingredients are walnuts, pine nuts and peanuts, which are often ground to make rich sauces.

A favourite drink is *pisco*, a grape brandy that is common to Peru and Chile. *Chicha*, a type of beer made from fermented corn, is also drunk.

STREET FOOD AND SNACKS

A popular snack is *anticuchos* (ox heart kebabs). The meat is trimmed, marinated in spiced vinegar and speared on lengths of sugar cane before being grilled with a spicy basting sauce. Other street foods include empanadas or *pastelos* (pastries stuffed with a variety of tasty fillings) and *humitas* (fresh corn dough with a savoury or sweet filling, steamed in a corn husk parcel). Crisp plantain chips are an Ecuadorian speciality, while Bolivians like to snack on caramel-coated popcorn called *pasacaya*.

FEASTS AND FESTIVALS

Easter is celebrated in style in all three countries. The best-known Quechua festival is Inti Raymi (the festival of the sun), which celebrates the winter solstice on 24 June each year. This huge celebration often continues for days. In Ecuador, the self-proclaimed banana capital of the world, there is a banana festival every September.

Below: In La Paz, Bolivia, a market trader displays just some of the many varieties of potato grown in the region.

CHILE

A slender ribbon of a country, Chile is dominated by the Andes mountain range and measures some 4,830km/3,000 miles from north to south, but is never much more than 160km/100 miles wide. In the north is the strangely beautiful Atacama Desert; in the south, beyond the Continental ice field, lies a rugged land of glaciers and fjords. Between these extremes is a temperate, fertile zone where fruits and vegetables grow abundantly. The waters off the coast of Chile provide superb seafood.

EARLY HISTORY

The north of Chile was once ruled by the Incas, but before they came to prominence in the early 13th century, the land played host to a succession of tribal groups. The first of these is believed to have settled in the south of the country as early as 14,000 years ago. More recent inhabitants were the

Below: Chile's ice fields, such as Torres del Paine, Patagonia, lie to the south of a more temperate, fertile area.

Aymara, who cultivated corn and potatoes in the far north, trading these foods for guano, a rich fertilizer gathered by coastal tribes. Also occupying the northern region were the Atacameño, whose descendants still uphold some of their tribal traditions. Another important group, the Mapuche, were fierce warriors who successfully kept the Inca and Spanish invaders at bay for centuries.

The Spanish finally gained a foothold in Chile in 1541, when Pedro de Valdivia founded Santiago. The town was almost lost six months later when natives attacked, but the community survived and less than 20 years later the Spanish were firmly entrenched.

The colonists quickly began to establish large estates or haciendas over much of the country. These were initially worked by native South Americans who were little more than slaves, but when the spread of European diseases virtually annihilated the native population, tenant farmers of mixed blood (*mestizos*) took their place.

Until the 18th century, Chile remained a largely agrarian country. As the Audiencia de Chile, linked for administrative purposes to the Viceroyalty of Peru, it was ruled from Lima, and was only permitted to trade with the mother country. All goods destined for Spain therefore had to go via Lima.

Chile was ripe for change when Napoleon's invasion of Spain in the early 19th century signalled the beginning of the end of that country's dominance in Latin America. When Napoleon placed his brother on the Spanish throne, the citizens of Santiago who were loyal to the deposed King Ferdinand VII refused to acknowledge the usurper, and declared on 18 September 1810 that they would rule Chile themselves until the French were ousted from Spain. This independence was short-lived, however, as troops from Peru soon re-established control. Independence would only be formally declared in 1818, after José de San Martin's liberation army had crossed from Argentina into Chile.

Above: Garlands of dried shellfish hang from market stalls in Puerto Montt, Chile, a town known for its seafood.

After initial turmoil, the country became relatively stable. Agriculture and mining prospered, and were bolstered by the arrival of settlers from Ireland, England, Germany, France, Italy, Croatia and the Middle East. All of these immigrants had an influence on the Chilean cuisine, but the national diet still has strong links with its origins, and traditional ingredients such as corn, squash, beans and potatoes are widely used.

FOOD AND DRINK

Any discussion about food in Chile inevitably centres on the extent, excellence and variety of seafood available. The plankton-rich Humboldt current is responsible for the largesse, which includes crabs, clams, mussels, abalone, razor clams, sea urchins, squid, octopus, scallops and lobsters. Some or all of these types of seafood, plus less identifiable specialities such as *picorocco* (giant barnacles), are likely to be among the treats on offer at that most Chilean of feasts, the *curanto*, a massive cookout that involves a carefully constructed pit, hot rocks and leaves to seal in the steam.

Fish is equally abundant. Popular varieties include congrio, a slender fish that resembles an eel; corvina, a type of bass; swordfish and the Patagonian toothfish. Chile is also one of the world's biggest exporters of salmon.

Corn features widely in many recipes, from soups and breads to the delicious *pastel de choclo*, which is a traditional stew topped with a corn crust. Meat is not as central to the diet as it is in neighbouring Argentina, but Chile produces some fine beef, pork and lamb nevertheless.

Chilean desserts are similar to those served elsewhere on the continent, mainly taking their inspiration from Spain and making great use of the thick, sweet caramelized milk called *dulce de leche*. The central valleys produce excellent fresh fruit throughout the year, and deliciously sweet cakes and pastries are also available, courtesy of German settlers.

Chileans enjoy a good bottle of wine and are extremely proud of their vineyards, which are rapidly gaining worldwide recognition. Also popular is draft beer, known locally as *schop,* and the delicious grape brandy, *pisco*.

A curanto on Chiloé
The beautiful archipelago of Chiloé, situated off Puerto Montt, is famous for its fine seafood, wooden churches and laid-back atmosphere. This is a great place to sample the *curanto* – a full-scale Chilean seafood feast.

STREET FOOD AND SNACKS

For munching on the move, Chileans tuck into meat, seafood, empanadas, *humitas* and sandwiches, from steak with all the trimmings to *ave-palta* (chicken and avocado).

FEASTS AND FESTIVALS

Independence Day on 18 September is celebrated with music, dancing, eating and drinking, and marks the start of summer. The rodeo season also starts in September, with the major event, the National Rodeo, taking place in March. Ngillatun is an ancient Mapuche festival celebrating harvest and fertility.

Below: An impressive array of fresh fruit and vegetables are on offer at a market in Valdivia in Chile's Lake District.

COLOMBIA AND VENEZUELA

At the upper end of South America lie two countries that are as mysterious as they are magnificent. Colombia and Venezuela have some of the most rugged terrain on the continent. From the tropical rainforest of the coast, the land rises to range after range of high mountains, the cordilleras of the Andes. Ravines, mighty rivers and dense vegetation make exploration difficult, and communities have historically been isolated. Until the first settlers arrived there was, therefore, no universal style of eating, and the Spanish were able to establish theirs as the core cuisine in both countries.

EARLY HISTORY

Columbus discovered the mouth of the Orinoco River in 1498. The first Spanish settlement in Venezuela was established in 1521 and in Colombia four years later. In the early 19th century both countries united with Ecuador and Panama to form the union of Gran Colombia, after their independence was won by Simon Bolivar. Venezuela left the union to become a separate state in 1830, as did Ecuador, and Panama eventually left the union in 1903.

FOOD AND DRINK

Both Colombia and Venezuela have lowland plains, temperate zones above 900m/3,000ft and highlands leading to alpine-style meadows. At sea level, sugar, cacao, coconuts, bananas and rice are cultivated. Higher up are the coffee plantations and corn fields, and above these cereal crops, potatoes and temperate fruits are all grown. This huge diversity of landscape means that both countries have a wide range of foods available to them, from the traditional ingredients such as cassava, squash, beans and corn to a dazzling array of fruits.

Favourite Venezuelan dishes include delicacies such as *mondongo* (tripe with vegetables, corn and potatoes), *sancocho* (fish stew) and *parrillado* (barbecued meats), while Colombian specialities include rabbit in coconut milk, chicken hotpot with three different types of potato, and a delicious

pineapple custard. Colombia has the benefit of a coastline on both the Caribbean Sea and the Pacific Ocean, so it has a wonderful selection of fish and seafood readily available. *Arepas* (flat corn breads) are a very popular snack. Both countries produce lots of coffee and it is one of their major exports; Colombian coffee is reckoned to be among the finest in the world.

Above: Roadside vendors are a common sight in Colombia, selling fruits such as bananas, melons and pineapples.

A seasonal speciality and a great delicacy in the lowland regions are flying ants, which are toasted and served like peanuts. In Venezuela a delicious spicy sauce, *katara*, is made from the heads of leaf-cutter ants.

The lure of El Dorado

The rumour of a land where gold was so plentiful that people powdered themselves with gold dust lured many 16th-century adventurers to the countries now known as Guyana, Surinam and French Guiana. The glut of gold never materialized but the Spanish, Dutch, English and French all thought that the land was worth fighting for.

The English eventually triumphed in Guyana, but only after many years of Dutch settlement. Surinam went to the Dutch and French Guiana became first a French penal colony and then an overseas department of France. Still heavily subsidized by France, French Guiana has a distinctly Gallic atmosphere, with pavement cafes and food with a distinctly French flavour. In Guyana and Surinam, where African slaves and indentured labourers from India, China and the East Indies were imported to work the sugar plantations, the cooking is more eclectic. Javanese noodle dishes and Chinese stir-fries are sold alongside native South American Indian dishes like pepperpot – a stew with meat tenderized by cassareep (cassava extract). Seafood is popular, especially prawns (shrimp), and plantains, bananas, cassava, beans, peanuts and squash are also widely used. The area is famous for its superb fruit, and for unusual vegetables like *pom*, a large yellow root that closely resembles cassava.

CENTRAL AMERICA

The land that connects Mexico with the rest of South America consists of seven countries, Guatemala, Belize, El Salvador, Honduras, Nicaragua, Costa Rica and Panama. Beans and rice are the staple foods in all these countries, but there is also fine fish to be had, thanks to the proximity of the Pacific Ocean and the Caribbean Sea.

EARLY HISTORY

The empire of the Maya extended to Honduras. When they disappeared from Central America around AD900 they not only left behind ruined cities like Tikal in Guatemala, but also new foods and sophisticated farming techniques, some of which were adopted by natives.

Columbus reached the shores of Honduras and then Costa Rica in 1502, but the area was not settled until some 20 years later, after troops led by Pedro de Alvarado came south from Mexico. Alvarado took Guatemala, Honduras and El Salvador. By 1530 there were Spanish colonists in most of Central America. Government was a haphazard affair, but in 1535 Guatemala, Honduras, El Salvador, Nicaragua and Costa Rica were incorporated into the Viceroyalty of New Spain, headquartered in Mexico City.

Below: Corn fields flourish alongside impressive mountains at the south-east tip of Lake Atitlan in Guatemala.

In 1821, the quintet opted out and two years later formed a federal republic, known as the United Provinces of Central America. The states were all autonomous, however. Belize became British, largely by default. Although the area was technically Spanish, British buccaneers established bases there and were later joined by British soldiers from Jamaica. In 1798 the British connection was formalized, and the link was only broken in 1981 when Belize became independent. Panama, meanwhile, looked to the south and was part of the Union of Gran Colombia until 1903. The building of the Panama Canal brought affluence to the area, and Panama is still one of the wealthier countries in Central America.

FOOD AND DRINK

The food of Central America is not as exciting as the surroundings, but competing against orchid-clad forests, volcanoes, waterfalls, barrier reefs and beautiful beaches would be a tall order. Dishes based on rice and beans are everywhere, but there are plenty of alternatives. Fish is universally popular. Varieties include tuna, mackerel, snapper, pompano, swordfish and mahi-mahi. The fish is often cooked simply and served whole, but there are also plenty of rich fish soups and stews. Lobsters, clams, prawns (shrimp) and

Above: In Costa Rica, a worker spreads out coffee beans to dry in the sun.

other types of seafood are also widely available. Chicken is always on the menu, alongside specialities such as *mondongo* (tripe stew) and *cecina* (beef marinated in citrus juices). There is a strong Mexican influence in Guatemala and Belize; Panama takes inspiration from Colombia; and Creole dishes are found on the Caribbean coast. Coffee is grown in Costa Rica, El Salvador and Guatemala and is enjoyed by everyone, from the very young to the very old.

Fabulous fruits

Central America is blessed with bountiful fruit. Markets throughout the region are filled with bananas, cherimoyas, mangoes, papayas, pineapples and guavas, plus many more varieties that are local to each country. Delicious fruit drinks are a popular choice. *Refrescos* or *frescos* are milk- or water-based, while *batidas* sometimes contain rum or a similar spirit. Also refreshing are *pipas*, large green coconuts that stallholders cut open on request so that thirsty purchasers can sip the cool liquid inside.

MEXICO

Most people tend to see typical Mexican cuisine as tortillas, tamales and tequila, but that is not strictly true. Mexico is a vast country, with an enormous range of unusual and delicious regional recipes, only some of which are represented in that synthesis of styles commonly known as Tex-Mex cooking. Many of the essential ingredients are only gradually becoming known outside the country, and the careful blending of flavours that is the mark of authentic Mexican cooking often comes as a delightful surprise to the uninitiated.

EARLY HISTORY

In ancient times, many different tribal groups occupied the area now known as Mexico. Most of these existed in isolation, hemmed in by lofty mountains or separated from each other by natural barriers such as deserts, jungles and canyons. On the central plateau and in Yucatan, two indigenous civilizations emerged that would have a considerable impact on the future of the country. The first was the Maya, whose empire stretched from Guatemala and Honduras to Yucatan, Chiapas and Campeche. The Maya had a complex society. They

Below: Workers sort through piles of newly picked avocados, a popular fruit used in many Mexican dishes.

used their knowledge of astronomy and mathematics to chart the heavens and built impressive stepped pyramids to their gods. They were also farmers, cultivating corn, beans, squash and chillies, including the bitingly hot habañero, which they used to make a sauce called *ixni-pec* (pronounced schneepeck) which is still popular today. A favourite flavouring was annatto (achiote) and they loved to drink chocolate. The Maya reached their zenith between AD600 and AD800, and by AD900 many of their ceremonial sites had been abandoned.

Not long after this, a tribe called the Mexica – better known as the Aztecs – began to emerge. By the beginning of the 14th century they had built a vast empire, with its capital at Tenochtitlán, where Mexico City is now. The city was magnificent, with gardens irrigated by water brought by an aqueduct from springs some distance away. Here successive emperors dined in splendour while their armies waged war on the surrounding tribes. Believing that the sun would only rise if regularly appeased with offerings of human hearts, the Aztecs sacrificed thousands of captives and earned a reputation for extreme cruelty. Their belief in the gods was to be their downfall, however, for when the Spaniard Hernán Cortes

Above: Cocoa beans were used to make chocolate, which was a popular drink among the ancient Aztecs.

reached their shores in 1519, they believed him to be the god Quetzalcoatl. When Cortes and his party reached Tenochtitlán, the Emperor Montezuma welcomed them, discovering too late that this was not a social visit. Within two years, the Spanish had totally subjugated the Aztecs.

For the next 300 years, Spain ruled Mexico, losing control only after Napoleon Bonaparte overran Spain in 1808. Mexico became an independent country in 1821, and a republic was set up in 1824, but this did not spell stability. In 1836 the state of Texas, which had been part of Mexico, declared itself an independent republic. When Texas joined the USA nine years later, the Mexican Civil War began, as a result of which Mexico ceded to the USA all territories south of the Rio Grande. The country has remained a republic ever since, apart from a brief period of French occupation between 1864 and 1867.

FOOD AND DRINK

The Spanish who invaded Mexico found a country filled with foods they had never seen before. Aside from corn, squash and unfamiliar beans, there were tomatoes, chillies, cactus paddles, tomatillos, avocados, jicamas, guavas

and pineapples. Turkeys, ducks and small hairless dogs were raised for the table, and runners brought fresh fish from the Gulf of Mexico every day, for Montezuma to feast upon. Corn was cooked in dozens of different ways. The common people consumed it as *atole*, which resembled porridge, or as tortillas, while the ruling class feasted on tamales. At the court of Montezuma, the emperor took his pick of hundreds of different dishes served at elaborate feasts. Although *pulque*, made from the fermented sap of the maguey cactus, was readily available, chocolate was the drink of choice for the Aztec elite.

The livestock that the Spanish brought with them revolutionized Mexican cooking. Cattle, goats, pigs and sheep were introduced. Milk, cheese, butter and eggs entered the diet, although they would never achieve the same importance in Mexico as they had in Europe. Pigs were used for lard, and lard made frying possible, which was a major step. Wheat, barley, citrus, olives, walnuts and grapes were planted, and other fruits and vegetables were introduced. Gradually, an entirely new style of cooking emerged.

Below: Small sugar skulls go on sale in early November to mark The Day of the Dead, a traditional Mexican festival.

The French occupation of Mexico left a legacy in the shape of delicious breads, crêpes, cakes and pastries. German settlers introduced brewing and expanded the local cheese-making, while recent immigrants from Asia and the Middle East have also had an impact on Mexican cuisine.

TYPICAL DISHES

Corn dishes are still hugely important in all but the north of the country, where wheat is more dominant. Tortillas form the basis of many *antojitos* (snack meals), but Mexican food has much more to offer. One example is *sopa seca*, the aptly named "dry soup" in which some of the moisture is soaked up by rice, vermicelli or strips of dry tortilla. On Pacific and Gulf shores, the seafood is outstanding, with sea bass, mackerel, swordfish and large prawns (shrimp) among the delights on offer.

Bean dishes have been popular in Mexico for millennia and *frijoles de olla*, pinto beans cooked slowly with water and a little lard, is not to be missed, especially if served with guacamole. Among the many meat and poultry dishes, *albondigas* (spicy meatballs) should be sampled, as should *chile verde*, pork in a green sauce with cactus paddles. Chillies are a central ingredient in the cuisine, and fresh and dried chillies are frequently blended to create dishes of great complexity.

Above: A typical Mexican street vendor sells fresh tortillas filled with beans, chillies, cheese and a variety of meats.

Custards and rice puddings, which are often very sweet, are the classic desserts. In contrast, fresh fruits are often served with salt, a sprinkling of chilli powder and fresh lime juice. Alcoholic drinks include locally produced wine and beer, tequila and mescal, and there is a wide selection of fruit drinks.

STREET FOOD AND SNACKS

Mexico has a handle on finger food. Neatly packaged burritos, tacos, tamales and *tortas* are all available from street vendors, as are *carnitas* – succulent pieces of pork cooked in orange-flavoured lard with garlic until the outside turns crisp.

FEASTS AND FESTIVALS

Most Mexican festivals have special foods associated with them. Epiphany, on 6 January, is celebrated with Kings' Day Bread, while The Day of the Dead at the start of November, when Mexicans honour their deceased relations, is marked by the eating of tamales, followed by a sweet pumpkin dessert and little sugar skulls. The traditional Christmas centrepiece is *mole poblano*, a rich turkey dish that brings together chilli and chocolate.

THE LATIN AMERICAN KITCHEN

Latin American cuisine is founded on simple ingredients of excellent quality. Fresh fish and shellfish, quality cuts of meat and locally grown exotic fruits and vegetables are abundant. Inevitably, each country has developed its own specialities, but there are common flavourings and techniques that are used throughout Latin America, creating a wonderfully varied cuisine.

EQUIPMENT

Latin American cooks are endlessly inventive, not only in the way they cook, but also in their approach to kitchen equipment. While the items featured here could give your cooking a more authentic touch, few are essential. If you intend making your own tortillas, a press and *comal* will be extremely useful, but for most purposes, it is perfectly possible to improvise.

METATE

Made from a sloping piece of volcanic rock and looking rather like a three-legged stone stool, this grinding stone is used to make *masa* dough from skinned, cooked corn kernels. It can also be used to grind cocoa and *piloncillo* (unrefined cane sugar). The grinding is done with the aid of a stone roller, a *muller*, which is made from the same stone as the *metate*. Before a new *metate* can be used, it must be tempered. A mixture of dry rice and salt is placed on the grinding surface, and the *muller* is rocked back and forth to press the mixture into the surface and remove any loose pieces of sand or grit. These are fairly difficult to obtain outside South America, but they are available by mail order.

Below: A metate *is a traditional grinding stone made from volcanic rock. The design has not changed for many centuries.*

MOLCAJETE AND TEJOLOTE

The Mexican mortar, the *molcajete*, is traditionally made from volcanic rock and must be tempered in the same way as the *metate*. The short, stubby pestle used to grind ingredients is called a *tejolote*. The best *molcajetes* are heavy and not too porous. Before purchasing, grind the *molcajete* briefly with the *tejolote*. If the stone seems soft and a lot of dust is formed, it is probably too porous. Similar to the Thai equivalent, which it closely resembles, it is ideal for grinding herbs, garlic, chillies and other spices such as achiote (annatto), as well as nuts and seeds for making *mole poblano*, for example. Fresh salsas, such as guacamole, are often made with a *molcajete* and *tejolote*. The flavours of the ingredients are crushed out, which gives a rustic texture and flavour. However, grinding spices or pounding chillies with a *molcajete* and *tejolote* is hard work so many Mexican cooks use a food processor or a blender instead.

Above: A mortar and pestle, or molcajete e tejolote, *is an essential tool for grinding spices and chillies.*

TORTILLA PRESS

In Mexico and other parts of Latin America where tortillas and similar griddle cakes are made, the *masa* dough was traditionally shaped by hand. Skilled women were able to make an astonishing number of perfectly shaped tortillas in a very short time, but this is something of a dying art. Today, most people use tortilla presses, and in tortilla bakeries or *tortillerias* the whole process is mechanized. The most effective tortilla presses are made from cast iron, but because these must be seasoned (oiled) before use, and carefully maintained, many people prefer steel presses. Tortilla presses consist of two round metal plates, hinged together. They come in various sizes and are heavy, in order to limit the leverage needed to work them. The dough is placed between the plates, which are then squeezed together with the aid of a lever. Placing thin sheets of plastic on the plates or covering them with plastic bags before making the tortillas will ensure that they are easy to remove once they are pressed. Tortilla presses are sold in good speciality kitchen shops and are also widely available by mail order.

Right:
Tortillas can be
easily pressed
with a heavy steel or
cast-iron tortilla press.

CUSCUZEIRO

This looks a bit like a metal colander supported on a frame, and it is used as a mould for the popular Brazilian dish *cuscuz paulista*. The *cuscuzeiro* is lined with a variety of foods that will look

EARTHENWARE DISHES

The Spanish influence on the region's cuisine is clearly visible in the clay pots (*ollas*) that are traditionally used for cooking stews and sauces throughout Latin America. Often beautifully hand-painted and decorated, they give food a unique earthy flavour, but are seldom found outside the region, as their fragility means that they do not travel well and are rarely exported. Sadly, modern materials and designs have made them relatively rare in Latin America itself. Flat earthenware dishes decorated around the edge are more easily found, and these are often used as serving dishes. Traditional Spanish *cazuelas* (shallow terracotta dishes) and casseroles also make excellent alternatives.

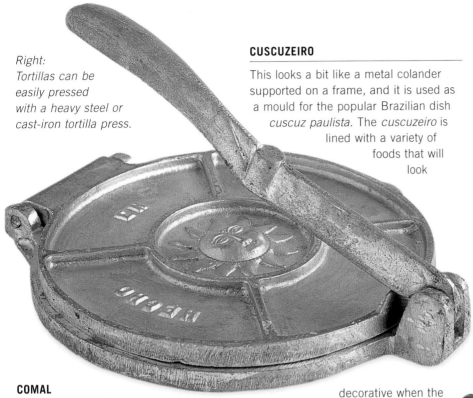

COMAL

This is a thin circular griddle, traditionally used over an open fire to cook tortillas. They were placed among the hot coals and pulled out with long sticks. Clay *comals* take longer to heat up, but they do not require oiling before use, unlike metal ones. If you cannot find a *comal*, a cast-iron griddle or large frying pan will do the job equally well.

FARINHERRA

This is a traditional shaker used mainly in Brazil for sprinkling *farinha de mandioca* (cassava flour) over meat or fish dishes, such as *feijoada*, to mop up the sauce and juices.

decorative when the dish is turned out, for example, slices of tomato, hard-boiled eggs or slices of pepper, with perhaps a few fresh prawns (shrimp). A moist corn meal mixture is then packed on top of these ingredients. More layers are added until the container is full, and it is then covered and steamed. When turned out the layers of the *cuscuz* look pretty and it tastes delicious. The name suggests that *cuscuz* evolved from couscous, and the method of preparation certainly calls to mind the North African dish.

Above: For slow-cooking rich stews and sauces, Latin American cooks often use ollas, *traditional hand-decorated Spanish clay pots, which give an authentic flavour.*

Left: Available as metal or clay varieties, a comal is the traditional griddle pan used for cooking tortillas.

CORN

The Aztecs called it "first mother and father, the source of life". Corn was equally highly revered in Peru, first by the indigenous South Americans, who worshipped the corn goddess, and then by the Incas, who decreed that corn could only be planted after the Supreme Inca had turned the first sod with a golden plough reserved for this purpose.

Corn was a sacred food, of huge significance. Not only was it a vital source of sustenance, but it also provided shelter, fencing and even clothing. Every part of the plant was used, even the silks surrounding the kernels, which became ties for tamales. When corn was cooked, whoever added it to the pot had first to breathe on it to rid it of its fear of dying and accustom it to the heat.

Some corn was eaten fresh, but most was dried and stored, then processed to make a type of porridge called *atole*. This was a lengthy chore, made easier by the discovery that the skins came off much more easily if the kernels were heated in a lime solution. When boiled in fresh water, the skinned kernels made a mash (*pozole*), versions of which were eaten by the indigenous peoples of Central and South America.

The cooked skinned kernels were also the basis for *masa*, a dough made by crushing the corn. The dough was then transformed into tortillas or similar flat breads, using techniques that are much the same today.

Corn is a valuable carbohydrate food but it is deficient in the amino acids lysine and tryptophan. If corn is the sole food source, as in some parts of Africa, diseases such as kwashiorkor and pellagra result. The problem has not arisen in South America or the Caribbean, however, because the basic diet also includes beans and squash, which compensate for the nutritional deficiencies of corn.

History

Corn evolved in Central America but its precise origin is not known. No wild forms have ever been found, and its ancestor may have been a type of grass with tiny kernels, each embedded in a cob no bigger than a haricot bean. How the grass evolved into the much larger plant with rows of kernels growing side by side on a substantial cob is not known, but the indigenous farmers were highly efficient plant breeders.

Corn was already widely grown throughout South America when Columbus first encountered it on the island of Cuba. The tall, leafy plant was called *maïs*, and

Above: White Andean corn is ground and used to make masa *dough.*

Below: South American corn comes in many colours, including vibrant red.

in many parts of the globe it is still known as maize. The alternative name arose because Columbus and his crew saw it as a staple food equivalent to the corn they grew back home, and dubbed it native corn.

Varieties

There are five main varieties of corn. Dent corn is the most widely grown globally, and is mainly used for animal feeds and oil. Other varieties are popcorn, flint corn, flour corn and sweet corn, which is the type used in cooking. Baby sweet corn cobs are often picked before they are mature, then cooked and eaten whole. Yellow corn kernels are the most common, but the corn grown in South America comes in other colours too, including red, blue, purple and the pale white that is typical of the Andean region. There are even variegated types available, which have sweet white, red

Above: Corn, known as mais, *is a native South American crop.*

and purple kernels on the same cob. For flavour, one of the most highly prized varieties is Peru's purple corn, *maiz morado*, which has a subtle citrus flavour and is used to make *mazamorra*, a delicious pudding, or the unusual drink, *chicha morrada*.

Buying and storing

If possible, corn should be cooked within 24 hours of being picked. This is because the sugar in the kernels starts to turn into starch as soon as the cobs are cut. Look for husks that are clean, shiny and well filled. If you are not sure whether the corn is ripe or not, take a look at the tassels, which should be golden brown. Unless you are planning to cook the corn the minute you get home, do not part the green husks to check out the contents; once the kernels have been exposed to the air, they will quickly begin to dry out.

Preparing corn

Corn can be cooked in many different ways, but when served as an accompaniment is usually simply boiled.

1 Strip off the green husks surrounding the cobs.

2 If only the kernels are required, lift the cob slightly and slice downwards using a sharp knife to remove a few rows at a time.

3 Whether using whole cobs, slices or just the kernels, plunge the corn into lightly salted boiling water for 4–5 minutes, until tender. Drain and serve with a knob of butter.

Huitlacoche

During times of drought, corn kernels are sometimes infected by a fungus, which turns them grey and causes them to swell to many times their original size. Far from being a disaster, this is seen as a boon, because the "corn truffles" as they are sometimes known, have a delicious, earthy flavour when cooked and are regarded as a delicacy around the world.

Cooking

Corn remains a staple ingredient in modern Latin America. Young, tender corn cobs are first stripped of their husks and then either steamed or cooked whole on a brazier or barbecue as a delicious fast-food snack. The puréed kernels also make an excellent soup. In Argentina, corn is often added to stews, such as the popular meat stew, *carbonada criolla*, while in Ecuador the kernels are mixed with salt cod and other vegetables to make the traditional dish, *fanesca*.

CORN MEAL

Also known as maize flour, corn meal remains slightly gritty when cooked, giving a characteristic texture to the flat breads for which it is most often used. The product known as cornflour in the UK and cornstarch in the US is a pure starch extracted from the grain. When mixed with regular wheat flour in a cake, it produces a lighter result. *Masa harina* is sometimes known as tortilla flour, which indicates its purpose. Although Latin cooks will often make *masa* (tortilla dough) from cooked corn kernels, the flour is an easier option. It comes in various grades, depending on what sort of corn it is made from. *Masarepa* is a similar product, used for making *arepas*, the flat griddle cakes that are popular in Venezuela and Colombia.

Right: Wet corn is ground to make masa harina, *which can then be used to make corn tortillas.*

Above: Dried corn husks should be soaked in cold water before use.

DRIED CORN HUSKS

These make handy wrappers for Mexican tamales and Peruvian *humitas*. They are fairly brittle, so should be soaked in water for about 30 minutes before being used to wrap ingredients. Dried corn husks are not always easy to obtain outside Latin America, so baking parchment can be used instead.

RICE

After its introduction to Central and South America by the Spanish in the 16th century, rice rapidly became a staple food crop. Large tracts of wetlands are given over to rice production, especially in Brazil, which grows as much rice as Japan. Rice is an important source of protein and carbohydrates for the poorest sector of the population, especially in urban areas where individuals spend 15 per cent of their income on white rice.

In Brazil, rice is an essential accompaniment to almost all main meals, particularly the national dish, *feijoada*, and is often layered in a mould with many other ingredients. In Peru, Colombia and Ecuador, where cooked rice is served quite dry, its granular texture earns it the name *arroz graneado*. Rice is also used to make drinks, such as the Mexican *horchata* and Ecuador's fermented rice drink, *arroz fermentado*.

Varieties

White long-grain rice is the variety grown throughout Latin America, although the influence of immigrants means that other varieties are imported.from overseas. White rice has been fully milled to remove the outer husk from the inner kernel, leaving a white grain with a delicate fragrance and slightly nutty flavour.

Below: White long-grain rice is served as an accompaniment throughout Latin America.

Buying and storing

Buy good quality rice in packets and store it in a cool, dry place. Rice keeps well, but once opened, it should be transferred to an airtight container. If cooked rice is cooled quickly, it can be stored for up to 24 hours in the refrigerator. Make sure it is piping hot before it is served next time. Don't reheat rice more than once, and never keep it warm for long periods because there is a risk of food poisoning.

Preparing rice

White long grain rice is fluffy and absorbent when cooked, and makes the perfect accompaniment to soups, stews and sauces. It may also be cooked with other ingredients to make a composite dish. If serving rice as an accompaniment:

1 Add 15ml/1 tbsp oil to a pan, heat gently, then add 1 clove of crushed garlic.

2 Add the rice to the pan and roast the grains for a few minutes until they begin to turn golden.

3 Transfer the rice to a pan full of lightly salted water. Bring to the boil, then add a tight-fitting lid and simmer gently until all of the liquid has been absorbed.

If the rice is to be mixed with other ingredients, for example in the Mexican dish, *sopa seca*, try the following method. It encourages the rice to absorb other flavours and reduces the final cooking time.

Quinoa

Indigenous to Peru, quinoa is a complete protein, possessing all eight essential amino acids. Low in saturated fat and high in fibre, it is a good source of calcium, potassium, zinc, iron, magnesium and B vitamins. Cooked like rice, the grain becomes soft and creamy, but the germ stays crunchy.

1 In a pan or heatproof bowl, soak the rice in freshly boiled water for 10 minutes.

2 Drain thoroughly before adding the other ingredients.

This fairly unusual method of cooking rice is very popular throughout the region, especially in Colombia, and is particularly delicious served with seafood.

1 Add 50ml/2fl oz/¼ cup coconut milk to a pan with a pinch of brown sugar.

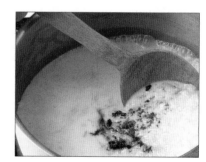

2 Add the rice, bring to the boil and simmer gently for 10–15 minutes, or until tender.

POTATOES

The potato is native to South America and was discovered by pre-Inca peoples in the foothills of the Andes. Archaeological digs in Peru and Bolivia have uncovered evidence that it was used as a food as long ago as 400BC. In Peru, the potato had religious significance, and the potato goddess was depicted with a potato plant in either hand. Potato designs were found in Nazca and Chimu pottery. One of the ways the South American Indians had of measuring time was to gauge how long it took to cook potatoes to certain consistencies. The Incas perfected the art of freeze-drying potatoes 2,000 years ago by leaving them out on lofty mountain tops to produce the early convenience food, *chuno*. In an entirely natural process, the night air froze the potatoes and the sun completed the lengthy dehydration process.

When the Inca empire was invaded by Francisco Pizarro in the 16th century, potatoes were among the plunder that the Conquistadors took back to Spain with them. Cultivation quickly spread throughout Europe via explorers such as Sir Francis Drake. Today there are up to 4,000 varieties worldwide. The potato is the staple food for two-thirds of the world's population and our third most important food crop.

Under the skin
Most of the nutrients in potatoes are either in or just beneath the skin, so it is best to avoid peeling potatoes if at all possible.

If you need to peel them, use a potato peeler that removes only the very top surface.

Potatoes are one of the best all-round sources of nutrition known to man. A valuable carbohydrate food, they also contain fairly high levels of protein. They are a very good source of vitamin C, a fact that was of huge value to early seafarers, who discovered that feeding potatoes to their crews helped to prevent scurvy. Potatoes also contain potassium, iron and vitamin B.

Varieties

In the UK, only about 15 varieties of potato are on general sale, but in Peruvian markets it is claimed that you can buy up to 100 different types, ranging in size from tiny potatoes to large ovals. Worldwide there are thought to be around 4,000 varieties. The colours are equally diverse, including red, black, yellow, brown, purple and black. Most are known only by their local names, but some are beginning to reach markets in the northern hemisphere. Look out for the Purple Peruvian, with its earthy, slightly nutty-tasting lavender flesh. Also prized, particularly for mashing, is the buttery Papa Amarilla, or yellow potato. Among the varieties with dark skins and dazzling white flesh are the Yanaimilla and the Compis. Potatoes will grow anywhere from sea level to 4,300m/14,000ft, so it is not surprising that so many different varieties continue to be cultivated in their place of origin.

Buying and storing

When buying potatoes, it is important to choose a variety that will give you the right results for the cooking method you intend to use. Check the labels or ask for advice from the seller. Store potatoes in a dark, cool, dry place. Paper sacks are better than plastic bags, which create humid conditions and hasten deterioration.

Above: Grown in Uruguay and Venezuela, the Red Pontiac has dark red skin and white waxy flesh.

Preparing and cooking

In Latin America, potatoes are usually either boiled in the minimum of water, as in the Peruvian speciality, *ocopa arequipena*, or diced and fried, which is a popular method in Mexico. Chillies are frequently added. Purple Peruvian potatoes are excellent in salads and they require less cooking than white or yellow potatoes.

Below: With striking dark skin and white flesh, Compis potatoes are grown by farmers in the Andean highlands.

BEANS

Along with corn and rice, beans are an extremely important food throughout Latin America. The inhabitants of Mexico and Central America eat around six times as many beans as are consumed in Britain every year, and in Chile, where meat can be relatively scarce, they are a vital source of protein. Beans are served, in one form or another, at most meals.

Several varieties of bean are indigenous to this part of the world. They were traditionally planted with corn and squash, the idea being that the corn stalks would support the growing beans, while the squash plants spread out to suffocate encroaching weeds. This ancient method of cultivation also ensured that the beans enriched the soil depleted by the corn. The beans were served fresh in season, but vast amounts were dried to furnish versatile and nutritious dishes all year round.

Beans are an excellent source of protein and carbohydrate and supply vitamins A, B1 and B2. They also contribute valuable amounts of minerals, such as potassium and iron, to the diet.

Below: Black beans are an essential ingredient in the extravagant Brazilian national dish, feijoada.

Varieties

Black beans These small, shiny, kidney-shaped beans, sometimes known as black turtle beans, are particularly popular in Mexico and Brazil. They are highly valued for their creamy white flesh and delicate earthy flavour, reminiscent of mushrooms. Their skins remain bright and shiny after cooking, so they look dramatic when combined with rice or other ingredients. Black beans are often used in salsas and soups, and are eaten as an accompaniment to Brazil's national dish, *feijoada*. In Costa Rica they are often fried with white rice to make the traditional breakfast dish, *gallo pinto*.

White beans A type of haricot (navy) bean, these vary in size but are always the same plump oval shape. When cooked, they have an earthy, rather floury flavour, and a fairly soft texture, but they retain their shape well. White beans are an extremely versatile ingredient and can be substituted for most other varieties when a recipe calls for dried beans.

Right: Native to Latin America, pinto beans are traditionally used to make refritos, *the Mexican speciality.*

Above: Versatile white beans, a type of haricot (navy) bean, are plump and soft with a delicious floury texture.

Pinto beans A smaller, paler version of the borlotti bean, the pinto has an attractive orange-pink skin speckled with rust-coloured flecks. One of the many relatives of the kidney bean, pinto beans are native to Latin America. They feature extensively in Mexican cooking as well as the cuisines of most other Spanish-speaking countries. The skins soften on cooking, which makes them easy to mash, so they are the perfect ingredient for the popular Mexican dish, *frijoles refritos* (refried beans).

Red kidney beans The shiny, dark red skin of these beans hides a pale interior. They retain their shape and colour when cooked and have a soft, mealy texture. Red kidney beans are particularly popular in Brazil and Mexico. Where they are frequently used as an alternative to the traditional pinto beans to make a variation on refried beans.

Lima beans These beans originated in Peru and are named after that country's capital city. Cream-coloured and tender, with soft flesh, these hold their shape well when cooked. Lima beans have a delicate flavour, similar to that of walnuts. Fresh lima beans are delicious. One variety of lima bean is the large white butter bean, which is familiar throughout Europe. Be careful not to overcook lima beans as they become pulpy and mushy in texture.

Black-eyed beans/peas Small and creamy coloured, with a distinctive black mark, these beans were introduced from West Africa. They need not be soaked before use because they rapidly become tender when cooked. They taste slightly sweet and readily absorb other flavours, especially in stews and curries. Add black-eyed beans to soups and salads for extra flavour. They can also be added to savoury bakes and casseroles.

Gungo peas Also known as pigeon peas, these are approximately the size of a garden pea. They have a sweetish, slightly acrid flavour, and are used fresh, canned or dried.

Chickpeas Also known as garbanzo beans, robust and hearty chickpeas resemble shelled hazelnuts and have a delicious nutty flavour and creamy texture, although they require lengthy cooking. Spanish migrants first introduced chickpeas to Latin America, and although they have never been as important or popular as native beans, they are now naturalized throughout the region. When fresh, they can be eaten raw or cooked, but they are more commonly available dried. The skin on chickpeas can be tough and you may like to remove it. Do this once the chickpeas are fully cooked and cooled.

Above: Chickpeas were first introduced to Latin America by Spanish settlers, but quickly became a popular ingredient.

Buying and storing

When buying fresh beans, buy young ones with bright, firm skins because the pods of older beans are likely to be slightly tough. Be sure to use fresh beans as soon as possible after purchase because they do not store well. Most fresh beans need little preparation other than trimming the ends, but older beans may need stringing.

When buying dried beans, look for plump, shiny beans with smooth, unbroken skins. Beans toughen with age and will take longer to cook the older they are, so although they will keep for up to a year in a cool, dark place, it is best to buy them in small quantities from a store with a regular turnover of stock. Avoid beans that look dusty or dirty, and store them in an airtight container in a cool, dark, dry place.

Canned beans are a useful standby as they require no soaking or lengthy cooking. Choose canned beans that do not have any added sugar or salt, and be sure to drain and rinse well before use. Canned beans still contain a reasonable amount of nutrients.

Preparing dried beans
Dried beans must be soaked before cooking.

1 Tip the beans into a colander or sieve (strainer) and pick them over to remove any grit or damaged beans.

2 Rinse the beans under cold running water and then drain.

3 Soak in cold water overnight, changing the water once.

4 Drain the soaked beans, rinse them, then place in a large pan with plenty of cold water.

5 Bring to the boil and boil vigorously for 10 minutes to remove natural toxins (this is particularly important with lima beans or red kidney beans).

6 Reduce the heat and simmer until the beans are tender.

COOK'S TIP
If you don't have time to soak dried beans overnight, put them in a pan with water to cover, bring them to the boil, then remove from the heat and leave to soak for about 1 hour.

CHILLIES AND SWEET PEPPERS

Chillies and their mild-mannered cousins, the sweet (bell) peppers, are without doubt Latin America's greatest contribution to the global kitchen. Full of flavour, colourful, nutritious and versatile, they are now so widely used in many different cuisines that it is difficult to imagine a world without them.

FRESH CHILLIES

The first chillies were tiny wild berries that grew in the South American jungle thousands of years ago. The plants gradually spread northwards from central South America through Central America and the Caribbean to south-western North America, evolving over the centuries into the wide range of shapes and sizes we encounter today.

It was Christopher Columbus who introduced chillies to the rest of the world. When he tasted a highly spiced dish on San Salvador, he assumed that its heat came from black pepper. He named the plant pimiento (pepper), and this name endured long after he realized his mistake. Columbus took chilli plants back with him when he returned to Europe, and by the 16th century they were widely distributed. Today the chilli is the most extensively cultivated and most commonly used spice in the world.

There are as many as 200 different varieties of chilli, varying enormously in shape, size, colour, flavour and, most of all, in the amount of heat they deliver.

Below: Poblanas, popular in Mexico, are often roasted to intensify their flavour.

Above: Scotch bonnet chillies are a very popular chilli and are used to make hot pepper sauce.

The fiery sensation from chillies is caused by capsaicin, an alkaloid that not only causes a burning sensation in the mouth, but also triggers the brain to release endorphins, natural painkillers that promote a sense of wellbeing and stimulation; this is why eating chillies can become quite addictive. Capsaicin is concentrated in the seeds and membrane of the pods, so removing these parts before eating will reduce the fieriness of a chilli considerably. Chillies are an excellent source of vitamin C and also yield valuable quantities of beta-carotene, folate, potassium and vitamin E. They stimulate the appetite, help improve circulation, and can also be used as a powerful decongestant.

Varieties

Of the vast range of chillies grown in Latin America the following are the most popular. They have been rated on a scale of one to ten for heat and are listed in order of potency, the mildest first. Be careful: the heat can vary widely, even with chillies from the same plant, so use these ratings as a guide only.

Left: Jalapeños and the smaller serrano chillies are either bright green or red, depending on ripeness.

Poblano These mild to medium-hot chillies (heat scale 3) are very popular in Mexico. Big and beautiful, poblanos are about 7.5cm/3in long, with thick flesh and a rich, earthy flavour. They start off dark green with a purple-black tinge and ripen to dark red. Green poblanos are always used cooked, and roasting gives them a more intense flavour. They are perfect for stuffed dishes such as *chillies rellenos* and taste good in traditional mole sauces. Dried poblanos are called anchos.

Jalapeño Well known and widely used the world over, jalapeños are medium-hot (heat scale 4–7). Plump and glossy, they are used in stews, salsas, breads, sauces and dips. Green jalapeños have a fresh, grassy flavour; red ones are slightly sweeter. Smoke-dried jalapeños are known as chipotle chillies. They are also very good when pickled.

Fresno Plump and cylindrical, these chillies are usually sold when red. They have thick flesh and a hot, sweet flavour (heat scale 5). Fresnos are excellent in salsas, ceviche, stuffings, bread and pickles. Roasting brings out their delicious sweetness.

Serrano Thin-skinned, quite slender and about the same length as jalapeños, serranos are the classic Mexican green chilli (*chiles verdes*) and are always used in guacamole. Although they are quite fiery (heat scale 7), they have a clean, biting heat, matched by a high acidity. Both red and green serranos are

Left: Sweet, juicy fresnos are perfect for fresh salsas or pickles.

frequently added to cooked dishes. They can also be pickled.

Aji mirasol Extensively used in Peruvian cooking, these chillies are narrow and tapered, with a tropical fruit flavour, yet they are decidedly hot (heat scale 6–7). Fresh yellow ones are particularly prized for salsas and ceviche. They are also used in cooked dishes, such as soups or stews, and are sometimes made into a paste, which is mixed with oil to make a hot dipping sauce.

Brazilian malagueta These very hot chillies (heat scale 8) are believed to be a wild form of tabasco. Very small, only about 2cm/¾in long, they have thin flesh and a fresh yet fiery taste. Malaguetas are often added to marinades and vinegars.

Jamaican hot Scotch bonnet and habañero These chillies are closely related and all are intensely fiery (heat scale 10). When cooking with any of these chillies, a little goes a long way. The Jamaican Hot is bright red and has a sweet, hot flavour. Habaneros are searingly hot, but if you can stand the heat they have a delicious fruity flavour and a surprisingly delicate aroma.

Below: Chilli powder is a good alternative when fresh chillies are not available.

Measuring the heat
The heat level of a chilli is often measured in Scoville units on a scale where 0 is the rating for a sweet (bell) pepper and 557,000 relates to the hottest chilli grown in Latin America, the habañero. The simpler system used in this book rates the chillies on a scale of one to ten, with one indicating the mildest and ten the hottest.

Preparing fresh chillies
Take great care when handling chillies, as the capsaicin they contain is an extremely powerful irritant. Wear rubber gloves while preparing chillies or wash your hands in soapy water afterwards. If you touch your skin by mistake, splash the affected area with cold water. Avoid scratching or rubbing inflamed skin because this could aggravate the problem.

1 Cut the chilli in half lengthways, cut off the stalk and carefully scrape out the seeds (unless you wish to leave them in for extra heat).

2 Remove the remaining core and any white membrane.

3 Finely slice or chop each piece, depending on use.

SWEET PEPPERS

Sometimes known as capsicums, sweet (bell) peppers are native to Mexico and Central America and were widely grown there in pre-Columbian times. Pepper seeds were carried to Spain in 1493 and from there spread rapidly throughout Europe. They also spread rapidly throughout South America and were a staple food of the Incas in Peru. They contribute colour and flavour to a huge variety of dishes, including salsas, stews and spicy meat fillings, as well as fish dishes, vegetable accompaniments and salads. Sweet peppers come in many unusual shapes and sizes, from chilli-size rounds to slender drops, bells and even hearts. Colours range from bright green, through yellow and orange to vibrant

Above: Delicious either cooked or raw, sweet peppers should look glossy, feel firm and have a crisp, juicy bite. Avoid those that are wrinkled.

red, and there is even a dark purple variety (but this does turn green when cooked). Mild and sweet in flavour, with crisp, juicy flesh when ripe, they can be eaten either raw in salads or cooked. A popular way of serving peppers is to stuff and bake them.

Buying and storing

Whether you are buying hot chillies or mild sweet peppers, look for firm, shiny specimens with unblemished skins. Avoid peppers that are limp, that wrinkle when touched or that have "blistered" areas on the skin. Green peppers should be purchased before they change colour, but should not be too dark as this indicates immaturity and lack of flavour. Avoid red peppers with dark patches on the skin, as this could be a sign that they have begun to rot inside. Store peppers in the vegetable crisper in the refrigerator. Sweet peppers will keep well for up to a week and chillies up to three weeks.

Preparing sweet peppers

Depending on use, the core and seeds should usually be removed before cooking sweet peppers.

1 Halve or quarter the peppers, then, using a small, sharp knife, carefully cut out the core, any white membrane and the seeds.

2 If the peppers are being used whole, for example to be stuffed, cut around the stem and pull out the seeds like a plug.

Roasting peppers and chillies

To really bring out the delicious, sweet flavour of fresh peppers and chillies, try roasting them.

1 Place them under a hot grill (broiler) and turn occasionally until the skins blister and char.

2 Alternatively, dry-fry them in a frying pan or griddle until the skins are scorched.

3 Place them in a strong plastic bag and tie the top tightly, or place them in a bowl and cover with cling film (plastic wrap).

4 After approximately 20 minutes, remove the skins, then slit each pepper or chilli. Remove the seeds and membrane, and tear or slice the flesh into pieces.

DRIED CHILLIES

Travel through Latin America and you will frequently see bunches of colourful chillies dangling from hooks on the walls of houses. In the bright sunshine they soon dehydrate and can be packed away until needed. When rehydrated, the chillies will not taste the same as before. In many cases they will have acquired a new intensity and richness of flavour, which is one of the reasons why Mexicans really value dried chillies and view them as distinct from the fresh, often giving them completely different names. Each variety has unique characteristics, and cooks will often blend several types to get exactly the results they require.

Varieties

The following are the most widely used varieties of dried chilli.

Ancho These dried red poblanos have a rich deep colour and mild fruity flavour (heat scale 3). Anchos can be stuffed and are often used in mole sauces.

Mulato Related to the ancho and with the same level of heat, mulatos taste smoky rather than fruity.

Guajillo These large dried chillies, orange-red in colour, have a slightly acidic flavour (heat scale 3–4).

Right: Habañeros are used for chilli sauces.

Below: Anchos are delicious stuffed or added to stews.

Left: Cascabels have a delicious, slightly nutty flavour.

Pasada Roasted, peeled and dried, these chillies have a toasty flavour (heat scale 3–4), with apple, liquorice and cherry notes. Used in sauces for meat and fish.

Cascabel The name means "little rattle" and refers to the sound the seeds make when the chillies are shaken. Thick-skinned and smooth, cascabels have a rich, woody flavour (heat scale 4).

Pasilla Long, slender and very dark, the flavour of pasillas is rich with hints of berries and liquorice (heat scale 4).

Chipotle Smoke-dried jalapeños, these have wrinkled dark red skin and thick flesh. Chipotles need long, slow cooking to soften them and bring out their full, smoky taste (heat scale 6–10).

Aji mirasol The dried version of Peru's favourite chilli is deep yellowish red with a berry-like fruit flavour (heat scale 6–7).

Pequin These small chillies are pale orange-red in colour, with a light, sweet, smoky flavour suggestive of corn and nuts (heat scale 8–9). They are excellent in sauces, salsas and soups and can be crushed over food as a condiment.

Habañero Used in moderation, these have a wonderful tropical fruit flavour (heat scale 10). Like dried Scotch bonnets, they are often used to make classic, hot pepper sauces, and are also good added to fish stews and salsas.

Above: Pasadas are often used in sauces for meat or fish, or in rich spicy stews.

Buying and storing

Dried chillies should be flexible. Avoid any that smell musty or have powdery skins, as this could indicate insect infestation. Store for up to 1 year in an airtight container in a cool, dry place.

Preparing dried chillies

To appreciate their full flavour, dried chillies should be soaked before use. Toasting dried chillies before soaking will give a lovely smoky flavour. If the chillies are to be used in a slow-cooked stew, soaking is not necessary.

1 Lightly dry-fry or toast the dried chillies in a frying pan or griddle for a couple of minutes.

2 Seed large chillies and tear into pieces, then soak in warm water until soft. Soak smaller chillies before cutting into pieces.

Hot sauces

Most regions have their own recipe for hot chilli sauce. Based on the fiery habañero or Scotch bonnet chilli pepper, they should be used sparingly by the uninitiated.

OTHER VEGETABLES

A visit to a market in any Latin American country is a real feast for the eyes. Fruit and vegetables are laid on mats or heaped high on tables, strings of chillies hang overhead and everywhere there are people bustling or bargaining. The colours are glorious, the aromas are unfamiliar and there will usually be several local specialities on sale.

CHAYOTES

Also known as christophenes, chokos or chow-chow, these pale green gourds are native to Mexico, where they are often used in salads and salsas. Raw chayote is crisp and clean-tasting, rather like water chestnut. The cooked vegetable has a rather bland flavour, so needs plenty of seasoning. Cholesterol-free and low in calories, chayotes are a good source of fibre and vitamin C.

Buying and storing

Choose smooth, unwrinkled chayotes and store in the refrigerator. They keep well but are best used as soon as possible after purchase.

SQUASH

Cultivated in Latin America long before Columbus sailed, squash is an important food. Many different types are eaten in Latin America, from courgettes (zucchini) to huge hard-skinned pumpkins. Squash are eaten in both

Below: Halved chayotes can be baked for a simple yet delicious side dish.

Preparing chayotes

Chayotes can be peeled, chopped and cooked in soups or stews, or cut in half and baked.

1 Preheat the oven to 190°C/375°F/Gas 5. Cut the chayotes in half, place them skin side down on a shallow baking tray and brush with a little olive oil.

2 Bake for approximately 25 minutes or until tender.

savoury and sweet dishes, often with brown sugar. Pumpkin and prawns (shrimp) is an unusual but delicious combination. A hollowed-out pumpkin makes a good container for cooking and serving, as in the Argentine stew, *carbonada criolla*. A good source of fibre and carbohydrate, pumpkins are low in calories. Varieties with bright flesh are high in vitamin A.

Buying and storing

If buying courgettes or other summer squash, the general rule is that the smaller the specimen, the better the flavour. Store courgettes in the refrigerator and use as soon as possible. Thanks to their hard skins, unbruised pumpkins and other winter squash keep well. Cut pumpkin should be wrapped in clear film (plastic wrap) and stored in the refrigerator.

Roasting squash

Instead of roasting, pieces of squash could be lightly boiled or steamed and added to stews.

1 Preheat the oven to 190°C/375°F/Gas 5. Cut the squash into wedges, remove the skin and seeds.

2 Place the wedges in a large roasting pan with a little olive oil and roast for approximately 45 minutes or until tender.

Below: Pumpkins can be easily stored over the long winter months, making them a popular ingredient all year round in many Latin American countries.

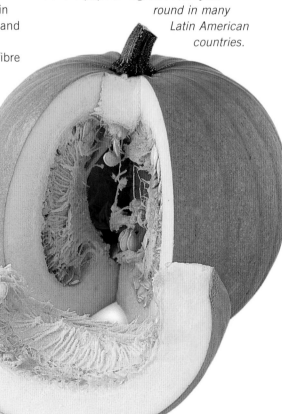

Above: Thin slices of sweet potato are fried to make chips, a popular street snack throughout Latin America.

SWEET POTATOES AND YAMS

These root vegetables are not related, although the American habit of calling red sweet potatoes yams can lead to confusion and the two are sometimes mixed up. Sweet potatoes have been grown in South America for centuries. In pre-Inca times, sun-dried sweet potato slices were a popular treat and Mayan cooks also used the vegetable to provide a sweet note in many savoury meat and fish dishes. Yams were originally brought to South America by African slaves and are widely used throughout Brazil. Both of these vegetables provide some vitamin C, while orange-fleshed sweet potatoes also contain beta-carotene.

Varieties

There are hundreds of varieties of both sweet potatoes and yams. In Latin American cooking, the red-skinned sweet potato with white flesh is best known. The most commonly used yam is brown, with moist cream-coloured flesh that becomes dry when cooked.

Buying and storing

Buy vegetables that are firm and dry, with no soft areas. Store loose or in a brown paper bag in a cool, dry place, but do not put them in the refrigerator.

Preparing and cooking

Like regular potatoes, sweet potatoes can be scrubbed and baked in their skins, or peeled and sliced, then boiled or fried. They are delicious mashed or creamed, and make very good chips. Yams must be thickly peeled and should be washed well before and after slicing; this helps to remove any toxins that may be present in the raw tuber. Always cook yams very thoroughly.

CASSAVA

Also known as *manioc, mandioc* or *yuca* (in Peru), this starchy tuber looks like a long, fat sausage with dark, rough outer skin. Native to Brazil, it is also a popular ingredient in West Indian cooking. It is important to distinguish between sweet and bitter cassava: the root and leaves of the former can safely be eaten, but bitter cassava contains cyanide. Although bitter cassava is used for making beer, tapioca and cassava flour – *farinha de mandioca* – it must be detoxified first. Sweet cassava is a carbohydrate food with a high fibre

Below: Sweet cassava is a versatile tuber and can be cooked in many ways.

content, and the leaves are a valuable source of protein. *Cassareep* is a delicious syrup made from cassava and flavoured with cinnamon and cloves. It is an essential ingredient in the traditional Jamaican pepperpot stew. Cassava is fairly bland so it is best served with a sauce or dressing such as the traditional Cuban *mojo*, which is a mixture of oil, citrus juices and garlic.

Buying and storing

Most cassava that is exported around the world is first coated in a layer of wax to keep it fresh. When buying sweet cassava, look for roots that are fairly firm, dry and odour-free.

Preparing cassava

An extremely versatile vegetable, sweet cassava can be cooked in a number of ways.

1 Scrub the root, peel, then cut into fairly large pieces, removing the fibrous core.

2 Drop the pieces into a bowl of acidulated water to prevent discoloration.

3 Boil, steam, bake or fry the cassava pieces until tender.

PALM HEARTS

The terminal bud of the Acai or cabbage palm has long been considered a regional delicacy. Native to South America, this fast-growing palm is now widely cultivated in vast plantations, mainly in Brazil and Costa Rica. Fresh palm hearts make very good eating, but are rarely available outside the country of origin. Canned palm hearts have a slightly different texture to fresh, but are still delicious and make a good alternative. Low in saturated fat and cholesterol, palm hearts are a valuable source of vitamin C.

Buying and storing

Fresh palm hearts should be pale, moist and evenly coloured. To enjoy them at their best, use as soon as possible after purchase. Canned hearts are much more readily available.

Preparing and cooking

To prepare fresh palm hearts, simply strip off the outer layers. Eat them raw or roast or steam in the same way as asparagus. Canned palm hearts are delicious in soups, salads and pies.

Below: Canned palm hearts make a good alternative if fresh ones are unavailable.

Above: Look for okra pods that are firm, plump and smooth, but not too big.

OKRA

Also known as ladies' fingers, these pods ooze a sticky liquid when cut, which acts as a thickener in sauces. Okra was introduced to Latin America by African slaves and is an important ingredient in Brazilian cooking. A source of vitamin C, fibre-rich okra also contains folate, thiamin and calcium.

Buying and storing

Okra should be a fresh, pale green colour. Buy smaller pods and avoid any that are flabby, shrivelled or bruised. Store in the refrigerator and use as soon as possible after purchase.

Preparing and cooking

If cooking whole, trim the top of each pod. If destined for a composite dish, where the viscous liquid will act as a thickener, cut the pods into slices. Otherwise, leave whole. Okra can be steamed, boiled or fried. Try it Brazilian-style, with chicken and chillies. The Barbadian speciality, Cou-cou, combines okra with corn meal.

LEAFY GREEN VEGETABLES

A number of leafy green vegetables are on sale in Latin American markets, and many are available only in certain areas. The young tops of cassava and sweet potatoes are regularly eaten, as is amaranth, a chard-like vegetable esteemed by the Aztecs. *Callaloo* is the name given to the leaves of two related tubers that are used for a popular Caribbean soup. *Nopales* are the edible leaves of the prickly pear cactus, while bottled *nopales*, commonly known as *nopalitos*, can be found in specialist food stores.

Unusual tubers

Jicama is indigenous to Mexico but has achieved widespread popularity thanks to its crisp, juicy flesh. Also known as yam bean or Chinese turnip, it can be eaten raw with orange juice and chilli powder, or cooked, and is especially good in salsas.

Oca looks like a short, fat wrinkled carrot. There are several varieties available, including white, yellow, red and purple. Its sharp taste is moderated by sun-drying the tubers before cooking.

Yacón, related to the Jerusalem artichoke, is highly valued in Peru and Bolivia for its sweet, crunchy flesh. It can be eaten either raw or cooked.

Añu is a white or yellow tuber from a nasturtium-like plant with edible leaves and flowers. It is an important crop in Ecuador, Peru, Bolivia, Colombia and Venezuela.

Jicama has crisp, juicy flesh, similar to green apples or water chestnuts.

FRUIT VEGETABLES

Neither savoury nor sweet, these are popular throughout Latin America.

TOMATOES

Along with chillies and corn, tomatoes are one of Latin America's most important contributions to the global cooking pot. Although they originated in the lands to the west of the Andes, both the Mayas and the Aztecs grew the little cherry-sized fruit vegetables and the Spanish introduced them to Europe. Largely composed of water, tomatoes are a good source of vitamins A and C. Raw ones contain useful amounts of vitamin E. Tomatoes also contribute the powerful antioxidant, lycopene, which may help to lower the risk of cancer.

Varieties

There are hundreds of varieties ot tomato. Cherry tomatoes, the closest in size to their Peruvian ancestors, are delicious in salads, juicy plum tomatoes make excellent sauces and beefsteak tomatoes are great for stuffing. Tomatillos (literally translated as "little tomatoes") are covered in brown papery husks. The fruit itself is green, with a clean, slightly acidic flavour.

Buying and storing

For the best flavour, buy tomatoes straight from the grower and store them at room temperature. Chilling tomatoes dulls their taste. Fresh tomatillos are difficult to obtain outside Latin America, but canned ones make a perfectly acceptable substitute.

Below: Fresh tomatillos are a tasty addition to spicy Mexican salsas.

Above: Tomatoes were enjoyed by the Mayas and Aztecs in ancient times.

Preparing and cooking

When adding to salsas and sauces, tomatoes should ideally have the skin removed. To skin tomatoes, cut a cross on the base, put them in a heatproof bowl and pour over boiling water. Leave for 30–60 seconds, then remove the remaining skin with a sharp knife. In Mexico, tomatillos are used fresh and raw, mostly in salsas, but they also taste great cooked.

AVOCADOS

The most nutritious of all the fruit vegetables, the avocado is native to Mexico, where it is called *acuacate*. In Brazil it is known as *abacate*, and in the US, alligator pear.

Nutrition

Despite the hefty calorie content – half an avocado delivers around 143kcals – the fat they contain is mostly mono-unsaturated and is a valuable source of energy. Avocados are protein-rich and also contain vitamins E, C and B6, plus copper and iron.

Varieties

Among the many varieties, some with soft, smooth skins, others encased in dark, wrinkled shells, the avocado with the best flavour is the hass, a dark avocado with buttery, golden yellow flesh.

Buying and storing

Obtaining the perfect avocado can be a tricky business. Some supermarkets package the fruits with a "ready to eat" label, which is helpful if the avocados are hard-skinned. To test if a soft-skinned avocado is ripe, press the top end gently – it should just give. Ripe avocados can be stored in the refrigerator; unripe ones should be put in a paper bag with a banana to soften.

Preparation and cooking

Avocados soon discolour when cut, but sprinkling the cut surface with lemon juice will help prevent this. To halve an avocado, run a knife lengthways around the fruit, cutting in to the stone (pit), then ease the halves apart. Remove the stone and peel the halves before chopping the flesh. The most common use for avocados is in guacamole, but they also taste wonderful in soups and mousses. Avocados are seldom cooked, but in Latin America slices are often added to soups or stews just before serving. In Brazil, avocado is served as a creamy dessert, *creme de abacate*.

Below: Although high in calories, avocados contain healthy fats and plenty of vitamins and minerals.

FRUIT

Some of the world's most colourful, exotic and intensely flavoured fruits are to be found throughout South and Central America.

PINEAPPLES

The taste of a freshly picked ripe pineapple is incomparable. Their aroma is so intense that a single pineapple can perfume the entire house, and the flesh is so sweet that it is unnecessary to add sugar or any other sweetener. Cultivated in Central America long before the arrival of Columbus, this majestic fruit has become popular the world over. Costa Rica and the Dominican Republic are the major producers. Pineapples are used in both sweet and savoury dishes and make refreshing drinks. In Venezuela and Columbia, pineapple is used as a popular flavouring for sweet custard desserts. Rich in vitamin C and a valuable source of fibre, pineapples also contain bromelain, a protein-digesting enzyme that soothes digestive complaints.

Varieties

There are hundreds of varieties of pineapple, ranging in size from the small "baby pineapples" to specimens 30cm/12in long. Some turn a deep golden yellow as they ripen, while others remain a bronze-green colour. The latest varieties to be cultivated are deliciously sweet and juicy.

Below: Papaya is a popular addition to Latin American fruit salads.

Above: Pineapples can be used to make a delicious refresco or fruit drink.

Buying and storing

Choose firm, ripe fruit with no bruising. The leaves should be glossy and fresh, and there should be a distinctive pineapple aroma. One test of ripeness is to gently pull a leaf from the bottom of the plume; if it comes away easily, the pineapple is ripe. Store whole pineapples in a cool place, but not the refrigerator, and use them as quickly as possible. Slices or cubes of pineapple should be stored in an airtight container and chilled in the refrigerator, where they will keep for up to three days.

PAPAYAS

These Latin American natives were slow to gain popularity in Europe. Before careful packaging techniques and speedy air travel ensured that the fruit reached its destination in good condition, the papayas on sale throughout Europe were far from their best

Preparing pineapple

The fruit is usually served fresh and raw, but cooking brings out the sweet flavour still more and pineapple tastes particularly good in hot, spicy dishes. Avoid using fresh pineapple in gelatine-based desserts, as the bromelain will prevent it from setting.

1 To grill (broil) pineapple, cut the fruit into quarters, remove the core from each piece, then loosen the flesh by running a sharp knife between the flesh and the skin, as when preparing melon.

2 Douse liberally with rum, sprinkle with brown sugar and place under a hot grill (broiler) until caramelized.

3 To cube pineapples, quarter the fruit, then remove the core and skin from each quarter, taking care to cut out the peppery "eyes". Cube the wedges or cut them into sticks.

– hard and unappetizing or soft and squashy. Today, the situation has improved considerably and more and more people are now beginning to appreciate the sweet, scented flesh of this delicious fruit. Papayas are extremely easy to digest, thanks to an enzyme, called papain, which they contain. Papain is a natural tenderizer, a fact that was well known to the pre-Colombian Indians who often marinated their meat in papaya juice to improve the quality. Amply stocked with vitamins A and C, and calcium, papayas are also a valuable source of fibre.

Below: Julie, one of more than 300 varieties of commercially cultivated mango, has sweet, tender flesh and an intense perfumed fragrance.

Preparing mangoes

Ripe mangoes are juicy and can be messy to eat. For convenience, cut the fruit into cubes or strips.

1 Cut a broad slice from either side of the mango, removing the "cheeks" or plump sides.

2 For long pieces, peel the skin from each cheek, slice the flesh lengthways, then cut off any flesh still sticking to the stone (pit).

3 To dice mango, leave the flesh on the skin and use a sharp knife to mark it into neat squares.

4 Gently press the mango cheek back on itself so that the pieces stand proud. Either eat straight from the skin with a spoon or use a sharp knife to slice off the chunks.

Varieties

All papayas are pear-shaped, but the size varies considerably, with some weighing up to 5kg/11lb or more. The skin starts off green, before ripening to a bright yellow or red. The sweet, scented flesh can be either pink or yellow. A hybrid form of papaya is the *babaco* from Ecuador, a fruit that can be served fresh or cooked. Stewed *babaco* tastes particularly good with roast meats.

Buying and storing

Look for small, soft papayas with undamaged, yellow skins. Handle them gently and use them as soon as possible. Store ripe papayas in the refrigerator; unripe papayas will continue to ripen at room temperature.

Preparing and serving

Cut the fruit in half and scoop out the seeds. The flavour of papaya is often improved with fresh lime juice in Mexico where chopped chillies might also be added to this tasty combination. Papaya can also be combined with coconut milk to make a soothing drink. The unripe fruit is also used in savoury dishes.

MANGOES

While many exotic native fruits have been transported from Latin America to European countries, mangoes made the journey in the opposite direction. These delectable fruits originated in Asia, but were enthusiastically embraced by Central American farmers as soon as they were introduced. The meltingly tender flesh, with its unique fragrance and flavour, makes mangoes a popular choice for drinks, desserts and even some savoury dishes. Ripe mangoes are a good source of fibre and they contain generous amounts of vitamin C. The vibrant orange flesh also makes them a valuable source of beta-carotene.

Varieties

Over 300 varieties of mango are commercially cultivated, with many more being grown in tropical gardens. One of the most popular varieties imported into Europe from the Caribbean is Julie. This medium-sized mango, slightly flattened on one side, comes mainly from the islands of Jamaica and Trinidad and Tobago. It contains only a small amount of fibre and is particularly noted for its fine flavour. Two other favourites are the kidney-shaped Madame Francis, which originated in Haiti, and the Brazilian Itamarica. Of the fibreless varieties, the Jamaican Bombay Green is highly regarded, as is Brazil's Mango de Ubá.

Buying and storing

Not all mangoes turn yellow or become rosy-cheeked when ripe, so colour is not necessarily a clear indication of ripeness. Avoid fruit with dark patches on the skin as this is a sign that the fruit is past its best. A perfect mango will have an intense sweet aroma and will yield when lightly pressed. Unripe mangoes will quickly ripen if placed in a paper bag with a banana.

Above: Guavas are used to make the delicious sweetmeat dulce de guayaba.

GUAVAS

Native to Central and Southern America, guavas were introduced to Europe by the Conquistadors. Brazil remains a major producer of these highly perfumed fruit, known as *guayabas* in Mexico. Guavas are usually used in desserts, but their flavour is such that they are equally good in savoury dishes, especially with fish. Guavas are an excellent source of vitamin C, better than most citrus fruits. They also contain vitamins A and B$_6$.

Varieties

The fruits can be oval or round, with shiny skin that turns pale yellow when ripe. Some varieties have creamy white flesh, while others have pink or even

Below: Grapefruits are native to Latin America.

purple flesh. Guava flesh has a clean, sweet, slightly acidic flavour, and a rather musky scent, but this disappears when the fruit is cooked.

Buying and storing

Look for firm, fairly small fruit that has ripened to a uniform yellow. Avoid any that are bruised or pockmarked. Wrap them well to avoid contaminating other foods with their musky odour, and store them in the refrigerator.

Preparing and serving

If the guavas are young there is no need to peel them. Just wash the fruit, then slice it, removing the larger seeds. Older fruit will need to be skinned and seeded. Guavas can be eaten raw with a little sugar to bring out their flavour, or cooked. In Latin America, sweetened guava pulp is used to make *dulce de guayaba*, which is similar to *membrillo*, the Spanish quince "cheese".

CITRUS FRUITS

The only citrus fruit that originated in Latin America is the grapefruit. A descendant of the Polynesian pomelo or shaddock, it is said to have been cultivated on Barbados. Grapefruit is thought to be useful in helping to lower cholesterol. Oranges came from China and India, and were introduced to Latin America by early traders. Seville oranges are particularly popular in the islands – although too bitter to eat raw, they are widely used in poultry and meat dishes. Limes were also an early import, hugely valued because they helped to prevent scurvy. Limes grow well in Latin America and their juice is widely used. Its most famous function is as a marinade for raw fish; the

Dulce de guayaba

This sweet guava paste, popular throughout Latin America, is delicious served with a hard cheese such as Manchego.

1 Peel 1kg/2¼lb guavas, then half each guava and scoop the seeds into a bowl. Add 200ml/7fl oz/ scant 1 cup water and set aside.

2 Chop the guavas and put them in a large, heavy pan. Pour over water to cover, bring to the boil, then cover and simmer, stirring frequently, for about 2 hours. Strain in the juice from the guava seeds and stir well.

3 Purée the mixture in a food processor, then press through a sieve into a bowl. Using a cup measure, scoop it into a heavy pan, noting the number of cups. Add an equal number of cups of sugar and stir in 30ml/2 tbsp lime juice.

4 Stir over a low heat until the mixture reddens and becomes very thick. Pour into a shallow pan and smooth the surface. Dry out in a barely warm oven and serve in small squares.

Above: Limes grow well the region and are a popular ingredient, especially in Mexican dishes.

action of the acid on the protein cooks the fish. Lemons are used in Latin American cooking, but are secondary to limes. All forms of citrus fruit are low in calories and are good sources of fibre and vitamin C.

Varieties

Grapefruit may be white, pink or ruby. There is also a green-skinned variety with sweet flesh. Oranges are either sweet or bitter. There are many varieties of sweet oranges, including Valencias, which are juicy and seedless. Of the bitter oranges, Sevilles are the best known. In addition to being used in cooking, bitter oranges are the basis for several liqueurs, including curaçao. There are three main types of lime – Tahitian, Mexican and Key Limes. Mexican limes are fairly small but have a strong and aromatic flavour.

Buying and storing

The juiciest fruits are those that feel fairly heavy for their size. Choose those with firm skin, avoiding any that are damaged or wrinkled. This advice is especially relevant to limes because they perish more quickly than other forms of citrus fruits. Choose bright green limes with shiny skins that are unmarked by brown patches. Grapefruit, lemons and limes should be stored in a cool place or the refrigerator for up to 1 week; oranges have a slightly longer shelf-life and will keep well for up to 2 weeks at cool room temperature.

BANANAS

Introduced to Central and South America from Portugal in the 16th century, bananas rapidly became naturalized and are today a very important food crop in the whole region. In fact, in some areas, of the Caribbean, they are practically the only crop. A large proportion of the world's organic bananas come from this area, as well as from the Dominican Republic and Mexico. Bananas are convenient, nutritious, tasty and so easy to digest that they can be eaten by everyone, old or young. With high levels of potassium, bananas also contribute vitamins C and B_6. The carbohydrate they contain boosts flagging energy levels. Banana leaves are also a popular ingredient and can be used as an alternative to corn husk wrappers for Mexican tamales and similar wrapped dishes.

Varieties

There are hundreds of different varieties of banana, though few are identified by name. Most familiar in our stores are the common yellow curved bananas, but it is sometimes possible to buy the tiny Brazilian lady fingers or sugar bananas. Red bananas, which come from Ecuador, have orange flesh and taste particularly good when cooked.

Buying and storing

Bananas are harvested when they are still green. By the time they reach stores in the northern hemisphere they have begun to ripen, and most are at their peak after being allowed to ripen in a warm room for a day or two. The skin of the fruit will become progressively darker, and will acquire brown speckles, but even at this stage, the flesh will probably be perfectly good to eat. Do not throw away very soft bananas; they can be used to make banana bread.

Preparing and serving

There's nothing tricky about preparing a banana – simply peel back the skin and eat. If you want to eat half a banana, fold the skin back across the uneaten piece, wrap the fruit well and it will still be edible the next day. Bananas are delicious fresh but can also be cooked. A popular way of preparing them is to bake them, or cook them on the barbecue, with plenty of brown sugar and cinnamon and a dash of rum to caramelize.

Above: Bananas are an important crop in Latin America; much of the world's supply comes from plantations in these areas.

OTHER FRUITS

Central and South America is also home to some more unusual fruits, including the following.

Breadfruit This large green fruit has very starchy flesh with a texture similar to potato although its flavour is comparable to sweet potato. Although very ripe breadfruit can be eaten raw, they are more often served cooked. They can be baked, boiled or fried and are highly nutritious. They are available fresh or canned.

Cherimoyas Indigenous to South America, cherimoyas have delicious creamy flesh that tastes like a cross between banana and pineapple, with a texture similar to papaya. The skin and seeds should not be eaten. Varieties include custard apples and soursops. Allow to ripen at room temperature, and eat before the fruit becomes too squishy

Prickly pears These are the fruits of several varieties of Central American cactus. Popular all over South America, they grow wild and are also cultivated. Beneath the prickly, tough outer skin, the flesh is sweet and aromatic, with a taste similar to melon but even more subtle. Prickly pear flesh can be eaten raw with a squeeze of lime juice and a sprinkling of chilli powder to bring out the flavour. They can also be made into jelly or jam.

Right: Beneath the pink skin, the flesh of the prickly pear is vibrant red.

Above: Be sure to remove tamarillo skin before eating or cooking the tangy flesh.

Tamarillos Native to the west coast of South America, these shiny, bright red oval fruits are grown commercially in Argentina, Brazil, Colombia and Venezuela. The skin is very bitter and must be removed before the tangy flesh can be enjoyed. A tamarillo dip is the traditional accompaniment for *arepas*, the flat corn breads that are popular in Venezuela and Colombia.

Passion fruits These fragrant fruits come from Central and South America and the best-tasting variety is round and very dark-skinned. The greenish yellow pulp has an exquisite flavour and the seeds are edible, although some people prefer to remove them. Large yellow passion fruits that look rather like light bulbs are granadillas. These have greyish pulp and are neither as flavoursome nor as highly scented as passion fruits.

Above: Choose passion fruits with extra-dark skin as these are sweetest.

Plantains

These are a type of banana grown as a vegetable, but the name is also used for green sweet bananas. True plantains taste very bitter and must be cooked before being eaten. Treat them like potatoes – they are good when baked in their skins, or they can be boiled, mashed, baked or fried as chips. A popular snack is *tostones de plátano*, long slices of slightly under-ripe plantain that are partially fried, squashed or pounded flat, and fried again until brown and crisp.

Below: Fresh plantains are prepared and cooked more like a vegetable than a fruit.

N U T S

Nutrient-rich nuts are a huge part of the Latin American diet, and they appear in various guises, most commonly as a thickening ingredient in both sweet and savoury sauces.

Coconuts The Latin American cuisine relies heavily on coconuts. The liquid they contain is used to flavour drinks and desserts, while the dense nutmeat is a valuable ingredient in almost everything, including soups, seafood and meat dishes and desserts. It is used fresh, dried or as coconut milk or cream, which can be bought canned.

Cashew nuts These are the fruit of an evergreen tree. Each nut grows out of the bottom of a fleshy bulge, which is called a cashew apple. Although not technically a fruit, it closely resembles one, rewarding the picker with crisp, juicy flesh. The nuts themselves are toxic and shelling is a tortuous business, but when released and detoxified, they make a tasty snack and are also used in drinks and sauces.

Pecan nuts These glossy red-skinned nuts are cultivated in northern Mexico, where they are often used in recipes, that hark back to the French occupation in the 19th century. Pecan nuts have a very high fat content so should be eaten sparingly.

Below: Many Latin American desserts are based on coconut or coconut milk.

Pine nuts The nuts of several native pine trees, including the Chilean araucaria and the Brazilian parana pine, are used in Latin American cooking. All are highly nutritious.

Almonds were introduced to Latin America by the Spanish, who cannily added the caveat that they could not be grown on a large scale, thus ensuring that the trade with their native country continued. They are still largely imported, so are fairly expensive and tend to be saved for more extravagant dishes or special occasions. Almonds are still used to make traditional Mexican chocolate, while almond paste is the basis of the luxurious sweetmeat, *turrón*.

Below: Cashew nuts are eaten as a snack with a cold beer or caipirinha.

Left: Almonds are mainly imported from Spain, while pecans and walnuts are native.

Below: Peanuts are a popular ingredient in savoury dishes, particularly with poultry.

Walnuts are grown in the highlands of central Mexico. Their bitter-sweet flavour makes them a popular ingredient in savoury dishes as well as desserts. They taste delicious when baked with potatoes and chillies.

Brazil nuts are the seeds of towering trees that grow wild in the Amazon rainforest. Inside the large husks are around 20 nuts, packed tightly together. Very high in oil, Brazil nuts go rancid quickly when shelled, so crack them at the last minute.

Peanuts These are actually pulses rather than nuts, and they grow just beneath the soil. They have been cultivated in Peru for centuries and are a highly valuable food crop, contributing protein and fat to the diet. Peanut brittle, made with caramelized, sugar is a popular sweet treat in Brazil, where it's called pe-de-moleque (kid's feet). Savoury dishes include pork and potatoes in peanut sauce. Peanut oil and peanut butter are also used.

HERBS, SPICES AND FLAVOURINGS

Many of the herbs and spices used in Latin American cooking will be familiar to the foreign visitor. Bunches of thyme, basil, oregano, mint, parsley and coriander (cilantro) scent the air in city markets, and spices such as nutmeg, allspice and cinnamon add their warm aroma. Asian immigrants have introduced cumin, five-spice power and curry powder, but it is perhaps the local specialities that are of most interest to the food tourist: *epazote*, *palillo*, *guascas* and the fiery chilli pastes and dried chillies used in Mexican cookery.

THYME

Widely used, especially in Mexico and Colombia, this robust and fragrant seasoning herb lends its flavour to a wide range of dishes including sauces, marinades and pickled chillies. The dried herb is included in the dry rub that is used to flavour *carnitas*.

Pebre

This hot coriander and chilli salsa from Chile is delicious with meats.

1 Whisk 15ml/1 tbsp red wine vinegar with 30ml/2 tbsp olive oil.

2 Add 2–3 aji mirasol chillies, seeded and very finely chopped, 1 finely chopped small onion, 2 crushed garlic cloves and 75ml/5 tbsp water.

3 Mix well, then stir in 90ml/ 6 tbsp chopped fresh coriander (cilantro). Cover and set aside for 2–3 hours at room temperature to allow the flavours to blend.

Below: Thyme is a popular flavouring in many Colombian dishes.

CORIANDER/CILANTRO

Native to Europe, coriander is grown in South America too, and is hugely popular, especially in Mexico and the Bahian cuisine of Brazil. Fresh coriander leaves go particularly well with fish. Chilli clam soup and crab and coconut soup both owe their distinctive flavouring to this popular herb. It also goes well with avocado and is used in both guacamole and avocado soup. Mexican green tomato dishes inevitably include coriander.

Right: Use mint to flavour a refreshing quinoa salad.

Below: Coriander is an essential ingredient in the Mexican salsa, guacamole.

MINT

South America cooks delight in using herbs in innovative ways. Mint and seafood is not an obvious combination, but their use of this familiar flavouring in chunky prawn chowder works extremely well. Mint is also used to flavour drinks and salads.

INDIGENOUS HERBS

Annatto/achiote The hard red-orange seeds of a tropical flowering tree, annatto has long been used as a flavouring and natural dye. The dried seeds have a mild flavour, with a hint of orange blossom. Annatto oil, pressed from the pulp that surrounds the seeds, is a popular flavouring and colouring for meat, fish and vegetable dishes. In the Yucatán peninsula, annatto seeds are often ground with cumin and oregano to make an aromatic rub for meats, such as spiced roast leg of lamb.

Epazote Also known as goose-foot, this herb is as commonplace in South America as oregano is on the islands of Greece. The dried leaves are crumbled and sold in jars. *Epazote* is widely used in central and southern Mexico, especially in bean dishes. The taste has been compared to anis.

Palillo This is an indigenous Peruvian herb. Dried and ground, it has little flavour and is mainly used to give food an attractive golden colour. Turmeric can be substituted, but use only half the amount suggested, as the flavour of turmeric can be overwhelming.

Guascas In Colombia, this herb is so common that it is sometimes viewed as a weed. The essential flavouring of the national dish, *ajiaco*, a delicious chicken soup, it is fairly difficult to obtain outside the country, except in dried and ground form. There is no real substitute as the flavour is unique, although it has been suggested that fennel comes close.

Huacatay comes from a plant that is closely related to the marigold. Pungent, with a rather unpleasant flavour, it is very much an acquired taste.

Vanilla

Vanilla is the seed pod of a tropical climbing orchid, which is put through a lengthy drying process. It is prized for its highly fragrant aroma and fine, soft, sweet flavour.

Records depicting Aztec life reveal that they were familiar with vanilla, and there is also evidence that it was used in Mexico in the the 16th century as a flavouring for hot chocolate. Until the 1800s the spice was grown exclusively in Mexico.

Good quality pods are dark brown, waxy and malleable, vanilla is perfect for adding to desserts. If a vanilla pod is placed in a sealed jar of sugar the sugar will take on the delicate vanilla aroma and flavour.

Left: (Anticlockwise from top) Warm spices, such as allspice, cinnamon sticks, ground cinnamon and annatto (achiote) are popoular throughout Latin America.

SPICES

The most popular spices in Central and South American cooking are those with warm flavours, like cinnamon, cloves, cumin, nutmeg and paprika. Several of these flavours are combined in the aptly named allspice, which comes from a type of tree related to the myrtle. Allspice berries are dark brown. When dried they resemble peppercorns. Allspice berries are picked, dried and ground or used whole in Central and South American cooking. Whole berries add flavour to vegetables or fish that is being pickled, and they are also added to meat dishes. Sometimes the whole berries even appear in desserts and drinks

Vanilla is another warm spice. The pods come from a climbing tree orchid, which grows in parts of Central America. Added to warm milk or chocolate, they impart a sweet and fragrant flavour. If just the seeds are required, slit the pod lengthways and carefully scrape them out with a sharp knife.

SWEET AND SOUR

Ever since sugar was introduced to Latin America in the 16th century, sweetmeats (*dulces*) have been enormously popular. Elaborately shaped and decorated, they are an everyday indulgence, as are caramel desserts, such as the flan, which resembles a caramel custard, but sometimes contains pineapple or coconut. Many cooks use unrefined sugar to make treats like these, selecting either *piloncillo*, the dark-brown Mexican sugar, or *panela*, the Colombian version.

As a contrast to all this sweetness, bitter flavours are also highly valued. Angostura bitters, an infusion of gentian root and herbs on a rum base, is often used to add a tart note to fish and meat dishes as well as drinks.

Below: In Peru, Bolivia, Ecuador and Chile the cocktail pisco sour is flavoured with a dash of Angostura bitters.

DAIRY PRODUCTS AND EGGS

Dairy products came to Latin America relatively late, and although milk, cheese and eggs are important foodstuffs, they do not have as prominent a role as in Europe or North America.

CHEESE

Before the Spanish conquest in the 16th century, fresh milk was a rarity in Latin America. In Peru, indigenous llamas, vicuñas and alpacas that had been domesticated were occasionally milked, but cheesemaking was unknown until the arrival of Spanish missionaries. Nor did their presence spell instant conversion to cheesemaking since finding a ready supply of milk would remain problematic for some time. The native animals were deemed unsuitable and goats failed to thrive in the humid lowlands. It was only when dairy cattle were established in more temperate zones that cheesemaking was attempted on anything but a minor scale, and the monks who travelled with the conquerors taught local people.

Cow's milk was used to make *queso blanco* (white cheese) – the simple soft cheese that is now a familiar sight in most Latin American countries. In the upland areas where goats were farmed, some cheese was made, but sheep's milk was not used until fairly recently, when farmers in Chile began producing a sheep's milk cheese similar to that produced in the Pyrenées.

There are plenty of cattle in Argentina and Brazil, but they are mainly beef animals. Most of the cheese eaten in Brazil is imported, as the high humidity makes cheese production difficult. A fresh cheese – Minas Frescal – is made in the Minas Gerais region, north of Rio de Janeiro, together with a stretched curd cheese called Minas Prensado.

The influx of immigrants proved to be a trigger for cheese production in many parts of South America. In 19th century Argentina, homesick Italians developed a cheese that closely resembled Parmesan, Treboligiano, as well as a mozzarella-type cheese called Moliterno. Cheese similar to Edam and Gouda satisfied the longing of Dutch settlers on Aruba for familiar flavours.

Below: Queso anejo *is a firm, dry cheese – use fresh Italian parmesan if unavailable.*

In Mexico, the demand for more European cheeses led to local production of cheeses such as Gruyère, Camembert and Port Salut, as well as a version of the Spanish cheese, Manchego. However, soft white cheeses remain the mainstay of the industry.

Queso blanco Made in most Latin American countries and eaten throughout the region, this white cow's milk cheese is traditionally produced from skimmed milk coagulated with lemon juice. Soft and crumbly, it is often used on enchiladas.

Queso fresco As the name, which means "fresh cheese" suggests, this is not a cheese for keeping. Young and unripened, it is usually eaten within a day or two of being made. It is mild and light, with a grainy, slightly crumbly texture. *Queso fresco* is actually the generic name for a number of cheeses, all of which share several common characteristics. It is often used for crumbling on top of finished dishes such as scrambled eggs, cooked *nopales* or other vegetables or bean dishes as a tasty garnish. *Queso fresco* has a fairly clean, sharp taste and is a good melting cheese so it is often used in tacos and on other tortilla-based snacks. If you can't find it in your local supermarket, substitute a good-quality mozzarella or ricotta.

Queso anejo Meaning "aged cheese", this is the dried version of a feta-like cheese. *Queso anejo* is a sharp, salty and fairly firm grating cheese similar to Parmesan, which makes a good substitute. It is often used for sprinkling on top of enchiladas

Queso Chihuahua Similar to *queso anejo*, but less salty, this originally comes from northern Mexico. It resembles Cheddar, and medium Cheddar can be used as a substitute. Alternatively, use the popular American cheese, Monterey Jack, which originated as *queso del pais* (country cheese) and was introduced to California by Spanish missionaries in the 18th century.

Asadero This slightly tart-tasting cheese is sometimes called *queso Oaxaca*, after the place in Mexico where it was originally made. The name *asadero* means "roasting cheese". It is a fairly stringy, supple cheese that is at its best when melted. It is ideal for stuffing fresh chillies, sweet (bell) peppers or other vegetables or meats, as it is unlikely to leak out during cooking. If *asadero* is unavailable, the closest equivalent is Italian mozzarella.

Above: Asadero *melts very well and is perfect for stuffing vegetables and meat.*

Above: When chickens were introduced to Latin America by the Spanish, hen's eggs quickly became popular and were added to many dishes.

MILK

As is the case in Spain, fresh milk is quite difficult to come by in this part of the world because of the heat and humidity. As a result, long-life, evaporated (unsweetened condensed) and condensed milks have become more popular. The use of these treated milks is simply a practical solution to the problem of keeping milk fresh in the heat, but several delicious dishes have evolved that make the most of these treated milks as ingredients. The most famous of these is *dulce de leche*, an incredibly sweet, caramel-flavoured concoction that is so thick and creamy it can be spread on bread like butter or jam. *Dulce de leche* is enomously popular among Latin American children. A rich dessert popular in Latin America, tres leches cake or 3 milk cake also makes use of condensed milk.

Milk and cream are also used throughout the region in a similar way to in Europe – they are often combined with fruit to make refreshing drinks, added to rich desserts and used in many savoury sauces, stews and soups. Canned evaporated or condensed milk is nearly always used instead of fresh cream or milk in hot drinks, such as coffee and hot chocolate, adding a distinctive rich, thick sweetness.

EGGS

Until the Spanish arrived in Latin America, the only eggs eaten were those from game birds, ducks, wild geese, reptiles and insects. The Aztecs farmed wild turkeys, but although there is evidence of turkey eggs being used in religious festivals, the birds appeared to have been prized more for their plumage and meat. When chickens arrived on the scene, however, hen's eggs rapidly became a valued food, and today it would be hard to imagine Mexico without *huevos rancheros*, a complete egg-based breakfast, and *rompope*, a cinnamon eggnog; Brazil without *quindao*; or anywhere in Latin America without the traditional flan (caramel custard). Throughout the region, eggs are used in both sweet and savoury dishes. Hard-boiled eggs are often used as a garnish on top of stews or vegetable dishes.

Below: Milk and cream are often added to fresh fruit to make refreshing drinks.

Dulce de leche

Originating in Spain. This incredibly sweet, toffee-like dessert is a favourite with children throughout Latin America. Literally translated as "caramelized milk". It is traditionally made with milk and sugar but this version is much quicker to make and just as delicious.

SERVES SIX

INGREDIENTS
400g/14oz can condensed milk
400g/14oz can evaporated (unsweetened condensed) milk

1 Combine the condensed and evaporated milk in a heavy pan. Place over a medium heat and bring to the boil. Reduce the heat slightly and cook, stirring constantly, for 30–35 minutes until thickened and toffee-coloured. Use a relatively large pan, as the milk has a tendency to boil over.

2 Pour into a sterilized jar and seal. *Dulce de leche* will keep for months, but with time, the texture will alter and won't be as smooth.

FISH AND SHELLFISH

When it comes to fish and shellfish, citizens of Central and South America are spoilt for choice. Every country except Bolivia and Paraguay has a coastline. You might expect the widest selection of fish to be available to the island dwellers of the Caribbean, but the finest seafood actually comes from the coastlines of Chile and Peru, where plankton brought up from the Antarctic by the icy Humboldt current provides a rich diet for the abundant sea life. The rivers and lakes teem with fresh fish, and both trout and salmon are farmed. The following list introduces just some of the fish available in Latin America, chosen either because they are particularly abundant or make a significant culinary contribution.

FRESH FISH

Snapper Two varieties of red snapper are to be found in the tropical waters of Central and South America. The American red snapper, which has lean white flesh with a very good flavour, is bright red all over, even including the eyes and fins. Its relative, the Caribbean red snapper, tends to be slightly smaller and is distinguished by its yellow eyes and paler belly. All snappers are very good to eat, whether baked, grilled (broiled), poached, steamed or pan-fried. The sweet, delicate flesh goes well with many types of fruit and fruit vegetables, such as mango or avocado. Caribbean snapper is often simply stuffed and baked, and sometimes wrapped in strips of bacon to keep the flesh juicy and tender.

Below: Warm-water groupers tend to have fairly firm flesh, this is a versatile fish that can be cooked in many ways.

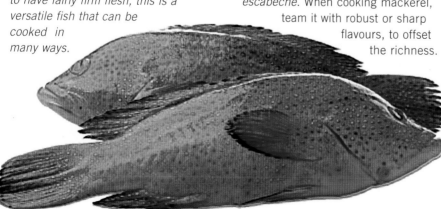

Mahi mahi/dolphinfish/dorade Of all the many names for this flavoursome fish, dolphinfish is perhaps the most unfortunate, since it leads people to imagine, quite wrongly, that it is related to the dolphin. The mahi mahi looks like no other fish. It has an unusual square head and a long, tapering body, which makes it look somewhat like a baseball bat. The firm white flesh of mahi mahi has a delicious sweet flavour.

Mackerel Several varieties of king mackerel are fished off the coast of Latin America, including the *cero*, which is fairly abundant in the Gulf of Mexico, and the *sierra*, which frequents Pacific waters. Mackerel are at their most delicious when eaten extremely fresh, and are a popular choice to be "cooked" with lime juice and eaten as *escabeche*. When cooking mackerel, team it with robust or sharp flavours, to offset the richness.

Left: Red snapper can be stuffed and simply baked or grilled for a delicious meal.

Sea bass These look rather like salmon, with elegant, slim bodies and silvery scales. Various species are found in the Caribbean Sea and the Pacific Ocean. Sea bass can be grilled (broiled), baked, braised, poached, fried or steamed, and they taste particularly good when combined with spicy flavours. In Peru, where the striped bass or corvina is preferred, the fish is cooked with chillies, while in Argentina it is often stuffed and baked.

Grouper These rather glum-looking fish, with their characteristic pouty lips, are members of the sea bass family. The warm-water groupers, such as those that are found in the Caribbean Sea, tend to have firmer flesh than delicate sea bass, and are good for poaching as well as frying, baking or cooking on the barbecue.

Patagonian toothfish This large fish is commonly known as the Chilean sea bass. It does come from Chilean waters, but the sea bass label is not accurate because it belongs to a separate species. Famed for its fine flavour, the Patagonian toothfish is popular in the US and Asia. There have been concerns about overfishing in recent years.

Buying fish

When buying fish, make sure that it is as fresh as possible. This is particularly important if you are intending to serve it as ceviche. Here's what to look for:

• There should be no apparent odour, other than a pleasant, faint smell of the sea.
• The eyes should be clear, bright and slightly bulging.
• The flesh should be firm and elastic; if you press it lightly with your finger it should spring back.
• The gills should gape, revealing a red or rosy interior.
• The scales should be firmly attached, not flaking off.

Swordfish are landed in the Gulf of Mexico and off the coast of Costa Rica from June to January and in Chile in late spring. The meaty flesh is low in fat and dries out quickly, so must be basted frequently if barbecued, or cooked in a sauce for the best results. Swordfish goes well with spicy flavours and Latin American cooks like to cook it with chillies and tomatoes. When buying swordfish, which is usually sold as steaks, check that the flesh is slightly translucent. It should be creamy white or pale pink, with the darker areas shading to a reddish-brown colour. Avoid steaks that look grey.

Pompano These are oily fish that taste similar to mackerel. They are available all year round, sometimes whole, but more often as fillets. There are several varieties in the warm seas off the coast of Central America, but the most common is the African

Left: Fresh trout are plentiful in Lake Titicaca, and are commonly eaten in the highlands of Peru and Bolivia.

pompano. This silvery, grey-finned fish has meaty flesh with a good, strong flavour. It is ideal for spicy dishes and goes well with chillies, coriander, red (bell) peppers and citrus fruit.

Congrio Found off the coasts of Chile and Peru, congrios resemble eels but are actually members of a distinctly separate species – *genypterus chilensis*. There are three types, all with firm, flavoursome flesh that flakes beautifully when cooked. This is one of the few fish to find its way into a poem. The Nobel prize-winning poet Pablo Neruda was so impressed with a bowl of congrio soup supped in his native Chile that he wrote an ode to the delicious fish.

Flying fish Also known as exocets, from which the name of the missile derives, these small fish really do look as if they are flying when you glimpse them leaping from the sea. Their propulsion comes from the tail and they stay in the air for several seconds, their pectoral fins giving them lift. When freshly caught and pan-fried, flying fish taste delicious. One method of preparation is to rub them with a mixture of garlic, herbs and hot pepper sauce before coating them in seasoned flour and frying them.

Above: Fresh swordfish steaks are delicious barbecued with a lime and chilli marinade.

Salt cod
Among the rations given to African slaves shipped over to work the sugar plantations was salt cod. They developed a taste for the rather unprepossessing looking food, and invented many recipes to make the most of its flavour. Some of these were based on those cooked by their Spanish or Portuguese masters, but they were often new. In Brazil, salt cod is served as a topping for baked eggs, while salt cod stew is a traditional Christmas Eve dinner in Mexico.

Below: Salt cod is used in many traditional dishes.

Trout There are plenty of trout in the cooler regions of Latin America. Rainbow, brown and brook trout are found in the Patagonian lakes close to Bariloche, and the icy rivers that flow from the Andes to the sea in Peru are also a magnet for trout fishermen. Lake Titicaca, on the Andean highlands between Peru and Bolivia, also has a plentiful supply of trout. Trout has a fresh, clean flavour and, although it is often cooked very simply – either fried or grilled (broiled) – more inventive chefs delight in introducing unusual flavour combinations. One particularly tasty dish combines spiced trout fillets with a rich wine and plantain sauce in a tasty Caribbean dish. The rosy flesh also looks lovely and tastes delicious when paired with fresh prawns (shrimp).

SHELLFISH

Latin America is a great place for shellfish. In the markets you'll not only come across familiar varieties, such as crabs and lobsters, but also rare and remarkable shellfish that look like algae-encrusted rocks, and sea urchins so large that their nickname – sea hedgehogs – seems entirely appropriate. Elsewhere in the region you can feast on conch, and in Brazil you can dine on some of the biggest prawns (shrimp) you are ever likely to encounter.

Crabs Both sea and land crabs are a delicacy in Latin America. There are many different varieties, from the soft-shelled blue crabs of the Atlantic and Gulf coasts to the mighty Patagonian king crabs. In Brazil, mangrove crabs are a great favourite, while Mexicans are partial to the California or Dungeness crab. Sweet and succulent, crab meat can be used in a wide variety of dishes. When carefully cooked, crab tastes good just as it is, but it also makes a great gumbo. Crab cakes are delicious. In Trinidad and Tobago, a favourite dish is a mixture of onion and crab meat in a rum sauce, served in crab shells.

Below: Crab meat is a Latin American delicacy, which can be added to soups or stews with other seafood.

Above: Tender king prawns are often grilled with fresh coconut for a popular Brazilian street snack.

Prawns and shrimp Several different types of prawns and shrimp are found in the oceans surrounding the continent. The biggest and best are probably the Gulf shrimp, which are found in warm waters. Sometimes pinky grey in colour but more often brilliant scarlet, these are big and succulent. Prawns are always included on a cold mixed fish and shellfish platter but also feature in cooked dishes. They are often cooked with fresh coconut or coconut milk, an unusual combination but one that works extremely well.

Dried shrimp Tiny shrimp, tossed in dendê oil and dried in the sun until crunchy, are popular throughout Latin America, but particularly in Brazil's coastal Bahia region. They give flavour and texture to soups, stews and salads, and are an essential ingredient in the Brazilian dipping sauce, *vatapá*. To prepare dried shrimp, rinse them under cold running water, then soak in hot water for about 35 minutes. They are often ground before being used.

Mussels On the west coast of the continent, where the sea is often turbulent, mussels cling tenaciously to the rocks until prised off by chefs or diners. They inevitably form part of the pit-cooked seafood extravaganza, the Chilean *curanto*, and are also used in a variety of soups and stews. Their sweet, tender flesh is nutritious and they taste best when lightly steamed. Before cooking mussels, it is important to discard any that are not tightly closed, or which do not close when tapped. The opposite applies after cooking, when it is those mussels that have failed to open that must be discarded.

Clams Among the hundreds of different clams found in Southern and Central America, perhaps the most delicious are the *navajuelas* (razorshells) found off the coast of Chile and Peru. These clams have tubular brown shells. When packed in bundles, they look like bamboo sticks, with the soft creamy flesh of the animal protruding from one end. Razorshells are often served raw, but can be cooked. More familiar hard shell clams include quahogs and littlenecks, which are often used in *chupes* (chowders) and angelwing clams, which are harvested in Mexico, Cuba, Puerto Rico and Chile.

Below: Fresh mussels are abundant in Chile, where seafood is plentiful.

Above: Razorshell clams, also known as navajuelas, *can be cooked but are more often served raw.*

Scallops Easily identified by their fan-shaped shells, scallops are a source of two delectable treats: the sweet, tender white meat and the bright orange roe or "coral". In Latin America, scallops are widely enjoyed, especially on the western seaboard. Black scallops, which are found off the coast of Ecuador, are especially sought after. Scallops are often eaten raw, with just a squeeze of lime, but they can be cooked. Keep the cooking time short, however – a couple of minutes at most.

A Chilean extravaganza

The ultimate South American seafood experience has to be the Chilean *curanto*, a sort of clambake but with a much wider selection of fish and shellfish, including squid, mussels and scallops. A fire is made in a large stone-lined pit. When the stones are hot, the fish and shellfish are placed on top and covered with leaves. The pit is then sealed and only opened hours later when everything is cooked to perfection. One of the best places to sample a real *curanto* is on the island of Chiloe, otherwise, try the one-pot version called *curanto en olla*.

Right: Really fresh king scallops have the best flavour.

Conch Pronounced "konk", this is the animal that lives inside those big, beautiful pink-lined shells that many people display in their bathrooms. A large relative of the whelk, conches are found in the warm, shallow waters of the Caribbean. The pink flesh is tasty and chewy and good to eat, whether raw or cooked, but it must be beaten to tenderize it first. The meat is often used in chowders, but is also good delicately fried. A favourite recipe is fresh conch fritters which are often served as a quick bar snack, alongside an ice-cold beer.

Abalone Like the conch, this is a gastropod, a sea creature with a single large foot for locomotion. Abalone feed exclusively on seaweed. They thrive in the cold waters off southern Chile, which are close to the world's largest kelp forests. Abalone are extremely difficult to prise from the rocks that they cling to, which helps to explain why they are fairly expensive. They are highly prized not only for their flesh, but also for their beautiful shells, which are lined with iridescent mother-of-pearl. Abalone has a delicious flavour but must be carefully prepared. Like conch, it needs to be tenderized carefully. Cynics sometimes suggest that the only way to do this successfully is to run it over with a truck, but beating with a wooden mallet usually does the trick.

Sea urchins There are over 800 species of sea urchin found all over the world, but only a few are edible. The ones found in Chile – called *erizos* – are unusually large, up to 10cm/4in across. Regarded as a gourmet delicacy, they are generally eaten raw. A tasty vinaigrette dressing may be offered, but lovers of sea urchins generally prefer them completely unadorned.

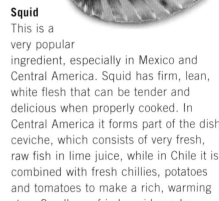

Squid This is a very popular ingredient, especially in Mexico and Central America. Squid has firm, lean, white flesh that can be tender and delicious when properly cooked. In Central America it forms part of the dish ceviche, which consists of very fresh, raw fish in lime juice, while in Chile it is combined with fresh chillies, potatoes and tomatoes to make a rich, warming stew. Small pan-fried squid can be found for sale along the coasts of South America as a delicious beach snack.

Below: Squid is a popular ingredient in Latin American cooking, with squid casserole a common dish in many areas.

MEAT

Visit Argentina, and you could easily imagine that South America was some kind of monument to meat, yet it was not always so. Before the 16th century, cattle, sheep and pigs were unknown on the continent and the only meat that was consumed came from wild boar, game birds, including the wild turkey, cameloids, small mammals, iguanas, snakes and some other reptiles.

BEEF

Fanning out from either side of the Rio de la Plata are the pampas, large grassy plains that are home to some of the finest beef cattle in the world. Stretching for thousands of miles, the pampas cover the temperate zones of Argentina and Uruguay.

It was the early colonists who introduced beef cattle to the region, along with the European grasses that soon supplanted native varieties. Those first cattle, with horses and other farm animals, were kept in compounds, but inevitably many escaped and, finding the pampas very much to their liking, multiplied to form the nucleus of what would eventually become vast wild herds. With both wild horses and cattle at large, it was only a matter of time before gauchos, the South American cowboys, tamed the one and set about capturing the other. Such private enterprise could not continue indefinitely, however. By the end of the 19th century, much of this cattle country was in

Below: Succulent thick rib joints are ideal for barbecuing.

the hands of private ranchers, and the gauchos had to work for them if they wanted to maintain their chosen way of life. Cattle farming became big business and today much of the world's supply of beef comes not only from Argentina but also from Brazil, Peru and Colombia. Large tracts of rainforest have been cleared to make way for new cattle stations; something that is of considerable and rising concern to environmentalists.

In Latin America, and especially in Argentina and Brazil, beef consumption is high. Argentines eat around one and a half times as much beef as Americans, with much of it cooked over coals, whether in restaurants or at outdoor *asados*. That the meat should be cooked to perfection is a matter of pride. Whole rib sections or flanks of beef are cooked vertically, speared on iron rods that are set at an angle to prevent the juices from dripping on to the fire. Smaller portions are laid out on barbecue grills, some of which are as big as table tennis tables.

A Brazilian speciality is the *churrasco* or mixed grill, which includes excellent beef steaks. Variations on this traditional dish are a feature of special restaurants called *churrascarias* that also specialize in spit-roasts. Pot roasts are a popular choice too, and there are scores of different recipes for rich beef stews, often incorporating chillies, chorizo or other sausages, fresh or dried fruit or even fish and shellfish. Vegetables that

Above: Beef topside is a lean, tender joint of meat, often used for braising or pot-roasting.

cook down to a purée, like potatoes and pumpkin, are often used for thickening sauces, or the delicious juices are mopped up with farofa, a form of toasted cassava flour. Beef is also used to make meatballs or as a tasty and often spicy filling for empanadas, *humitas* or tamales.

Dried meat

In the heat of Latin America, meat tends to go off fairly quickly, so before refrigeration was an option it was necessary to find ways of preserving it. Chief among these was drying, a method that remains popular to this day. To make *cecina*, beef or pork is salted and partially dried, then treated with fresh lemon juice before being briefly air-dried again. During the process the meat acquires a robust flavour, and when it is tenderized it makes extremely good eating. *Cecina* is used to add a rich flavour to stews or as fillings for tortillas and tamales. More thoroughly dehydrated meat is *charqui* or *jerky*, which is produced by air-drying strips of meat in the icy Andean winds. Also available is *carne seca*, the traditional sun-dried salt beef of Brazil, a version of which is also produced in Colombia.

Carnitas

These crisp morsels of marinated meat, usually pork, are a popular Mexican snack, especially in Bajio, to the north of Mexico City.

The meat is cooked in lard, with garlic and oranges, and has a delicious flavour. *Carnitas* are served with salsa as an appetizer or used as a delicious filling for tacos or burritos.

LAMB

The main sheep-farming areas of Latin America are Patagonia, in the south of Argentina, and Uruguay. Sheep are also to be found on the Paramos, the high plateaux between the tree line and the snow line in Chile and Peru. Although lamb and mutton have historically been

Below: Lamb is becoming more popular in South America and is often rubbed with a mixture of spices.

less popular than beef in Argentina, lamb is now gaining ground. Mutton and lamb are popular in Mexico and Central America, featuring in dishes such as spiced roast leg of lamb. A favourite way of cooking lamb is to marinate it in a mixture of garlic and warm spices, including ground annatto (achiote) seeds, then roast it with sweet (bell) peppers and beans. The annatto gives the meat a rich red colour.

PORK

When Spanish and Portuguese colonists introduced pigs to Mexico and other parts of Central and South America, there was jubilation, not just because the meat tasted so good, but also because the lard was such a valuable ingredient for cooking techniques such as frying and baking. Pork hasn't got the high profile and popularity that beef enjoys, but it is a popular meat, especially in Mexico where they produce the highly seasoned pork sausage Chorizo and in Brazil, where pork ribs, smoked tongue and pork sausage feature in the national dish, *feijoada*. In Argentina and Peru, meat is cooked in milk. Pork cooked in this way is very tender.

KID

In the upland areas where goats thrive, they are highly valued for their milk, meat and hides. Kid – young goat – has a slighlty more gamey flavour than lamb, but the two types of meat are often used interchangeably. The famous Jamaican dish, curry goat, is frequently made using lamb

Above: The top end of a pork leg is excellent as a joint for roasting.

instead, although the title makes it obvious that this wasn't always the case. As well as a slightly stronger flavour, kid is a little tougher than lamb, and therefore needs a longer cooking time for the best results.

Offal

Latin American cooks don't just eat offal, they celebrate it. Intestines, hearts, kidneys, tripe, pigs' feet – in fact all the animal parts eschewed in many other places around the world – are elevated to gourmet status by careful cooking with herbs, spices and sauces. Sausages of all types are also widely eaten, with chorizo being a particular favourite.

Below: Spanish-style chorizo and other dried sausages are often eaten in Latin America.

POULTRY

Although turkeys are native to Latin America and were first domesticated by the Aztecs, along with ducks, chickens were unknown until they were introduced by the Spanish and Portuguese colonists.

CHICKEN

As in many other places throughout the world, chickens can be found absolutely everywhere in Latin America: scratching in backyards, on sale at busy markets and on the menu at home and in restaurants. In some areas such as the nearby Caribbean, there is seldom enough land to raise large food animals, unlike on the vast plains of the Pampas, so chickens are a practical source of protein. Throughout Central and South America chicken is often baked in pies; simmered in soups and hot-pots; and cooked over the coals; or stewed in delicious hot-pots thickened with okra or peanut based sauces. All over Latin America, and especially in Peru, you can find simple spit-roasted chickens – pollos a la brasa – on sale.

Below: Every part of Central and South America has its own favourite chicken recipe.

Jointing a duck

When preparing a duck, it is important to remember that there is not a great deal of meat on these birds. The simplest and fairest way of serving it is in four equal-sized portions, so the duck must be jointed before cooking.

2 Continue cutting the bird in half, along either side of the backbone.

1 Place the whole bird, breast-up, on a chopping board. Remove the wing tips with poultry shears or a sharp knife and then cut the breast in half, working from the tail towards the neck.

3 Cut each piece of duck roughly in half, cutting diagonally.

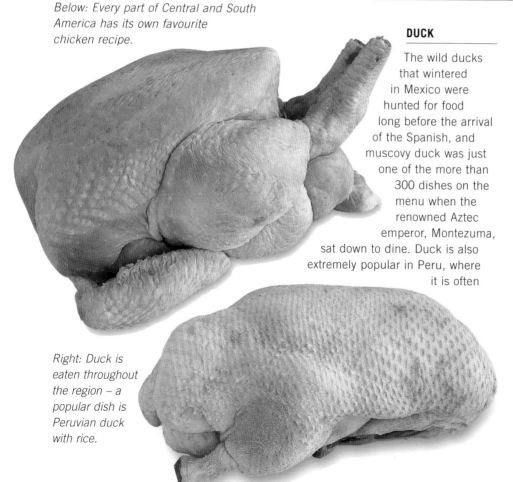

Right: Duck is eaten throughout the region – a popular dish is Peruvian duck with rice.

DUCK

The wild ducks that wintered in Mexico were hunted for food long before the arrival of the Spanish, and muscovy duck was just one of the more than 300 dishes on the menu when the renowned Aztec emperor, Montezuma, sat down to dine. Duck is also extremely popular in Peru, where it is often cooked with fresh coriander (cilantro) leaves. For lovers of duck, Latin America provides some delicious and unusual recipes, such as duck roasted with sweet potatoes and red wine, or cooked with rum.

TURKEY

Two types of turkey are native to Latin America, one emerging in Yucatán and Guatemala and the other in Mexico. Turkeys were introduced to Europe by the Spanish and they soon became a popular choice in France, Italy and Britain too. The wild birds were fast runners and strong fliers, and their bright feathers were highly prized for ceremonial head-dresses and jewellery, and to provide flights for arrows. The Aztecs were the first to domesticate wild turkeys, which they called huexolotlin. Aside from being a valuable food source, turkeys also had a strong religious significance, and two festivals were held every year in their honour. Probably the most famous Latin American dish

Above: Quails are very small birds – for a main course, serve two per person.

involving turkey is the Mexican *poblano mole*. There are many versions of this, all of which involve the bird being cooked in a thick, rich sauce, which contains numerous fresh or dried chillies and several pieces of rich, dark chocolate or cocoa powder. Turkey is often cooked with fresh fruit and tastes especially good with sweet, juicy mango.

GAME BIRDS

Wild birds were a vital part of the South American diet in the pre-Colombian era, and they are still hunted in many places today. Pheasant, partridge, quail and pigeon are all regularly eaten, along with several types of jungle bird, including some breeds of parrot. Pheasant is particularly good for roasting or stewing, young partridge is best simply roasted and served in their own cooking juices, while pigeon is delicious braised or cooked in a pigeon pie. The *curassow*, a large

black bird with a distinctive crest of curved feathers, can be found from Mexico to Brazil. It is widely regarded as being the best game bird in Latin America, and is therefore in high demand, a fact that has led to over-hunting. Sadly, it has become an endangered species in some areas.

EXOTIC AND UNUSUAL MEATS

In Peru, guinea pigs (*cuyes*) have long been a favourite food. Domesticated in much the same way as chickens, roaming around backyards, they are cooked by similar methods. The vegetarian diet of *cuyes*, like rabbits, gives their meat a fairly light, delicate flavour. Roast *cuy* is sometimes on the menu at out-of-town restaurants and is readily available roasted at many Peruvian markets and on street stalls, but it is more often eaten at home.

Deer are hunted in forest regions, as are *moufflon*, a type of wild sheep, *peccaries*, which are similar to pigs, and wild goats. Llamas and other large cameloids were often cooked and eaten many centuries ago. In certain areas, they occasionally still are, but they tend to be more highly valued as pack animals. Subsistence hunters catch agoutis, tapirs, armadillos, capybara, monkeys, snakes, iguanas and even tortoises. Turtles are also considered a delicacy and are occasionally eaten, although some countries have made their capture and trade illegal.

Above: Turkeys are native to Latin America and were bred by the Aztecs centuries ago.

Pheasant in green pipian sauce
This delicious recipe from the Yucatán peninsula can be used for almost any game bird.

SERVES 4

INGREDIENTS
30ml/2 tbsp oil
2 oven-ready pheasants, halved lengthways
1 onion, finely chopped
2 garlic cloves, crushed
275g/10oz can tomatillos
175g/6oz/generous 1 cup pepitas (pumpkin seeds), ground
15ml/1 tbsp annatto (achiote) seeds, ground
475ml/16fl oz/2 cups chicken stock
salt and ground black pepper
fresh coriander (cilantro), to garnish

1 Heat the oil in a frying pan and sauté the pheasant halves until lightly browned. Place them in a large roasting pan.

2 Purée the onion, garlic and tomatillos, with their juice, in a food processor or blender. Scrape the purée into a pan and add the pepitas and annatto seeds.

3 Stir in the stock and cook gently for 10 minutes, taking care not to burn. Leave to cool.

4 Preheat the oven to 180°C/ 350°F/Gas 4. Pour the sauce over the pheasant and bake for about 40 minutes, basting occasionally. Garnish with fresh coriander (cilantro) and serve immediately.

DRINKS

There are some delightful ways of slaking your thirst in Latin America, from sipping cool coconut juice or a refreshing fruit drink to sampling local wines and spirits. If the latter makes you sleepy, there is always strong coffee to wake you up, or a cup of chocolate to help you relax.

ALCOHOL-FREE DRINKS

Fruit drinks These are something of a speciality in many parts of Central and South America. *Sugos* and *refrescos* or *frescas* are always worth sampling and are particularly popular with children. Made while you wait, from whatever local fruit is available and in season such as pineapple, lime, citrus fruits and even tamarind, these fruit drinks tend to be on the sweet side. Ice helps to take the edge off, but they can be served without sugar if preferred. One unusual drink, which is very popular in Brazil, is *guaraná*. Made from the berries of a tree sacred to Amazonian tribes, the drink is sold in both still and carbonated forms and is credited with a vast range of health-giving properties. Guarana is similar to caffeine and is said to have the same sort of effects. It is available in powder form from health food shops.

Below: Fruit agua frescas are sold by street vendors all over Latin America.

The perfect cup
In Latin America, any time is the right time for full-bodied coffee, and visitors are often staggered by the strength of the brew and the amount consumed. To make a perfect cup, follow these directions:
• Use fresh, cold water that has not been chemically softened.
• Use 60–75ml/4–5 tbsp per 600ml/1 pint/2½ cups.
• Boil the water, then let it cool slightly before pouring it on to the ground coffee.
• If you are using a jug or cafetière (plunge pot) let the coffee stand for 3–4 minutes before pouring or plunging.
• Do not reheat coffee or keep it warm for long periods.

Coffee Two-thirds of the world's supply of coffee comes from Latin America and the Caribbean. Brazil is the leading grower and exporter, with Colombia second. Other important producers are Mexico, El Salvador, Guatemala, Costa Rica, Ecuador and Peru. Coffee is not native to Latin America, however. It was introduced, so the story goes, by a young naval officer called Gabriel de Clieu, who carried a small sapling with him when he sailed to the Caribbean from Europe in 1723. On the voyage, the ship was becalmed, but De Clieu used part of his own water ration to keep the sapling alive until he could plant it on his estate in Martinique. It was clearly a robust specimen, however, because in fewer than 60 years there

Below: Coffee beans must first be roasted before they can be ground.

were 18 million coffee trees on Martinique and production had spread to Central and South America.

There are about 50 species of coffee, but the only ones that are commercially significant are *Coffea arabica* and *Coffea canephora (robusta)*. *Robusta* likes humid, tropical conditions and grows well below 600m/1,900ft, while *arabica* prefers the heights and is cultivated between 600 and 2,000m/1,900 and 6,500ft. The young trees do best in well-drained volcanic soil. They need plenty of sun, but cannot tolerate excessively high temperatures, so shade trees are planted between the rows.

Coffee trees are beautiful. They bear jasmine-scented white flowers up to three times a year, and these are followed by the berry-like fruit. These start off green, but gradually ripen to red, when the cherries, as they are called, are harvested. After picking, which must be done by hand for coffee of the highest quality, the cherries go through lengthy processing to release the pair of beans hidden inside each. Before the beans can be ground to make coffee, they must be roasted. Coffee connoisseurs in Latin America like to roast and grind their own beans at home every day, but most of us buy our beans ready-roasted. In some countries, a light roast is preferred, while in others a dark roast is favoured.

Discriminating drinkers demand specific types of coffee, such as Colombian Medellin, but most of what is exported has been blended, either to appeal to the majority or to persuade us to buy coffee tailored to a time of day: light for breakfast and full-bodied for after dinner, for instance.

Yerba maté
This herbal tea, made from the leaves of a plant that resembles holly, is popular in Argentina, Uruguay, Paraguay and southern Brazil. It is traditionally sipped through a silver straw from a hollow gourd, the *maté*, from which it takes its name.

Above: Good-quality chocolate is still produced in Bariloche, Patagonia.

Chocolate The cacao tree is indigenous to Latin America. One fifth of the world's production now comes from Brazil, with Ecuador only 2 per cent behind. The Olmecs, who inhabited Central America around 1200BC, are credited with discovering that the cacao bean could be transformed into a delicious drink, but it was the Maya and later the Aztecs who perfected the art. For the emperor Montezuma, the perfect end to one of his legendary feasts was a gold cup full of the frothy beverage.

The Aztecs credited cocoa with medicinal powers, and used the drink to treat all sorts of ailments. In this they were ahead of their time, for cocoa has been proven to be high in antioxidants, the natural compounds that are widely believed to reduce cholesterol levels, fight cancer and heart disease and delay signs of ageing. The drink the Aztecs enjoyed was not sweetened, but the natural bitterness of the chocolate was often offset by adding chillies and other warm spices, such as vanilla.

The Spanish first introduced chocolate to the rest of the world and it was soon being drunk in sophisticated resorts and cities all over Europe.

Above: Hot chocolate is the perfect end to a meal, according to Montezuma.

Although it is now as a form of confectionery that chocolate is best known and loved in Europe and the US, its main use in Latin America continues to be as a drink. Mexican chocolate is a delicate mixture of dark and bitter chocolate, sugar, ground almonds and cinnamon, and it tastes incredibly rich.

Swiss chocolate, Argentine-style
Although chocolate is more likely to be a drink than a sweet treat in Latin America, there is one place where bars of very good chocolate are regularly produced, and that is the beautiful Lake District of Patagonia. Descendants of Swiss, German and northern Italian immigrants have established a thriving chocolate industry in Bariloche, with many locals hand-making their own chocolates. This Andean village is a visual delight, known for its mountains, its lakes and the European look of its streets. The thriving chocolate industry helps to reinforce the town's decidedly Swiss character.

WINE

Much of South America is too hot for successful wine production. However, in Argentina and Chile, in the cool valleys on either side of the Andes, grapes flourish and wine is produced widely.

Argentina is the world's leading wine producer outside of Europe and the US, coming fifth in the global line-up. Until recently, Argentines drank most of the wine they produced themselves, but this is gradually changing. Despite producing less wine than Argentina, Chile has a bigger bite of the international market, and produces some highly regarded wines. Wine is also produced on a smaller scale in Uruguay, Brazil and Mexico.

Argentina

The first vines were planted in Argentina in the middle of the 16th century by Jesuit priests eager to ensure a steady supply of communion wine, Gradually the vineyards became established, and the industry gained a useful boost in the 18th and 19th

Below: Parts of South America, particularly Chile and Argentina, are well known for both their red and white wines.

centuries with the arrival of European viticulturists. They introduced many of the varieties that continue to dominate: Merlot, Cabernet Sauvignon, Chardonnay, Chenin and Pinot Noir.

Most of Argentina's wine comes from the western part of the country, in an area stretching from Rio Negro in the south to La Rioja and Salta in the north. By far the most productive region is Mendoza, which has well over a thousand wineries, despite having very low rainfall. This is because the whole area lies in the rain shadow of the Andes. Paradoxically, however, it is thanks to the Andes that the grapes flourish, as the vines are fed by irrigation from snow and ice-melt.

It is for red wines that Argentina is best known. These include Cabernet Sauvignon, Syrah, Merlot, Malbec, Bonarda, Pinot Noir, Tempranillo and Sangiovese. Malbec is of particular interest. This black grape originated in France, but never fully realized its potential until it was introduced to South America. A wine with an intense, vibrant colour, Malbec has been described as having distinctive berry flavours, with hints of damson, liquorice and even chocolate.

Among the white wines produced are Chenin Blanc, Sauvignon Blanc, Chardonnay and Semillon, From the northern provinces of Salta and La Rioja comes Torrontés, a varietal that is believed to have Spanish antecedents, but which is now strongly established in its adoptive country. Fresh, fruity and deliciously dry, it is extremely popular.

Chile

Roughly one-third of the length of this slender ribbon of a country is given over to the growing of grapes. Although the northern part of the country is desert and the southern tip is too cold for wine production, the central temperate valleys have ideal conditions. The main wine-producing area stretches for just under 900km/550 miles from north of Santiago to Concepción. This part of the country has a Mediterranean climate similar to that enjoyed in South Africa's Western Cape, and because the

Right: Cuzco is a well known South American lager. It takes its name from the ancient Inca city in the high Andes of Peru.

moisture-laden clouds that roll in from the ocean drop their rain in winter on the Chilean side of the Andes, irrigation is not the problem it is on the other side of the mountains in Argentina.

Wine production began with the introduction of the rustic Pais grape to Chile in 1548, and owes its present character to the introduction of French vines in the middle of the 19th century. Established varieties like Cabernet Sauvignon, Cabernet Franc, Merlot, Malbec and Sauvignon Blanc soon flourished, and when European vineyards were devastated by a small insect – phylloxera – Chile was fortunately spared and made the most of this opportunity.

The Maipo Valley is the most famous wine-growing area of Chile and the site of some of the oldest established vineyards. It is well-known for producing excellent Cabernet Sauvignon. Also well known for reds are the Curicó and Colchagua Valleys, while some of the finest white wines come from the Aconcagua and Casablanca Valleys in the north. Mulchen, which is at the southern tip of the wine-producing region, is another white wine area, known especially for Sauvignon Blanc and Chardonnay wines.

Thanks to the huge north-south spread and a variety of microclimates, Chile has a wide range of both red and white wines, including several organic varieties. Aside from those varieties already mentioned, Merlot, Carmenère, Malbec, Syrah, Pinot Noir and Viognier are also successfully produced.

BEER

Best known for light, thin lager drunk straight from the bottle with a wedge of lime, Central and South American beer actually has a much richer tradition than is widely appreciated. The Mayans were brewing beer from fermented corn stalks long before Spanish conquistadors invaded, while, in northern Mexico, the Aztecs enjoyed a fermented drink made with sprouted maize. The Spanish settlers set up small breweries from the 16th century onwards, but beer came a poor second to distilled spirits, until German immigrants introduced lager to Mexico. Many of the brewing companies in existence today have German roots. Mexico remains the leading beer producer, with Brazil being the second-largest. Lager is the popular drink of choice in Latin America with most brewers offering a light pilsner. Well-known brands include Corona Extra, Cuzco, Dos Equis, Sol and Tecate. These lagers go well with spicy Latin American food. Other, more eclectic and traditional brews can also be found.

SPIRITS

Latin America has given the world some fine spirits, including rum and tequila.

Rum Legend has it that rum was discovered after sugar-cane mash was left to ferment in the Caribbean sun

Liqueurs
Some of the world's most popular liqueurs originated in parts of Central America and the nearby islands of the Caribbean. Curaçao, was the forerunner of Grand Marnier and Cointreau.
All are still made using oranges from the region. Kahlúa is a coffee liqueur made in Mexico city which is popular throught the world. It is added to fresh coffee to make an after dinner drink and is a popular ingredient in cocktails. Kahlua is delicious when drunk straight, with cream floated on the top and is also irresistible when combined with vanilla ice cream.

Above: Rum remains a popular spirit in South and Central America.

soon after the first sugar plantations were established on the islands in the 16th century. In the early 18th century, it became standard practice for the British Navy to issue sailors with a daily ration of rum, largely because the spirit endured extremes of weather so much better than beer. At the same time, rum was becoming popular in Britain. Over the centuries, the spirit has been refined, and aged rums now have the same sort of prestige as that accorded to single malt whiskies. Rum is still largely produced in the Caribbean, and some of the world's finest rums come from Jamaica, Cuba, the Dominican Republic, Martinique, Barbados, Haiti and the British Virgin Islands. Rum is also produced in South America.

Cachaça Another cane spirit, *cachaça* is distilled from the first crush of the sugar cane. Also called *pinga* or *aguardente*, it is the national drink of Brazil and is often

mixed with freshly squeezed lime juice and sugar to make the delicious and popular *caipirinha* cocktail, which is often enjoyed with meals.

Pisco A grape brandy, the birthplace of *pisco* is in some doubt. It originated either in Peru or Chile, depending on which of those countries your informant favours. Its one-time reputation for rough fieriness does not apply to the top grades of *pisco*, which have a delicate, fruity flavour.

Mescal and tequila A distillate made from the juice of the agave cactus, *mescal* is that pale yellow spirit that traditionally comes with a worm in the bottle, and many Mexicans appreciate its fiery qualities. Tequila, of which there are many varieties, is produced by putting the spirit through a second distillation process.

Below: Mexico's finest exports include mescal (left) and tequila blanco (right).

STREET FOOD
AND SNACKS

*Throughout Latin America there is a tradition of street food. Market stalls,
beach huts, bars and snack houses all offer sweet or savoury snacks, which make
perfect accompaniments to fruit juice, cold beer or cocktails.*

CORN TORTILLAS

To make these delicious Mexican specialities, make sure you have ready a tortilla press and a small plastic bag, cut open and halved crossways.

MAKES ABOUT FOURTEEN

INGREDIENTS
275g/10oz/2½ cups *masa harina*
250–350ml/8–12fl oz/
  1–1½ cups water

COOK'S TIP
Tortillas are very easy to make but it is important to get the dough texture right. If it is too dry and crumbly, add a little water; if it is too wet, add more *masa harina*. If you misjudge the pressure needed for flattening the ball of dough to a neat circle on the tortilla press, just scrap it off, re-roll it and try again.

1 Put the *masa harina* into a bowl and stir in 250ml/8fl oz/1 cup of the water, mixing it to a soft dough that just holds together. If it is too dry, add a little more water. Cover the bowl with a cloth and set aside for 15 minutes.

2 Preheat the oven to 150°C/300°F/ Gas 2. Open the tortilla press and line both sides with the prepared plastic sheets. Preheat a griddle until hot.

3 Knead the dough lightly and shape into 14 balls. Put a ball on the press and bring the top down firmly to flatten the dough out into a round.

4 Open the press. Peel off the top layer of plastic and, using the bottom layer, lift the tortilla out of the press. Peel off the bottom plastic and flip the tortilla on to the hot griddle.

5 Cook for 1 minute and turn over and cook for a minute more. Wrap in foil and keep warm. Repeat for the other tortillas.

FLOUR TORTILLAS

THESE ARE MORE COMMON THAN CORN TORTILLAS IN THE NORTH OF MEXICO, FROM SONORA TO CHIHUAHUA, WHERE WHEAT IS GROWN. FOR THE BEST RESULTS, USE A GOOD QUALITY PLAIN FLOUR.

MAKES ABOUT FOURTEEN

INGREDIENTS
225g/8oz/2 cups plain
  (all-purpose) flour
5ml/1 tsp salt
15ml/1 tbsp lard or vegetable fat
120ml/4fl oz/½ cup water

1 Sift the flour and salt into a large mixing bowl. Gradually rub in the lard or vegetable fat using your fingertips until the mixture resembles coarse breadcrumbs.

2 Gradually add the water and mix to a soft dough. Knead lightly, form into a ball, cover with a cloth and leave to rest for 15 minutes.

COOK'S TIP
Make flour tortillas whenever *masa harina* is difficult to find. To keep them soft and pliable, make sure they are kept warm until ready to serve, and eat as soon as possible.

3 Carefully divide the dough into about 14 portions and form these portions into small balls. One by one, roll out each ball of dough on a lightly floured wooden board to a round measuring about 15cm/6in. Trim the rounds if necessary.

4 Heat an ungreased griddle or frying pan over a moderate heat. Cook the tortillas for about 1½–2 minutes on each side. Turn over with a palette knife or metal spatula when the bottom begins to brown. Wrap in foil and keep warm in the oven until ready to serve.

CORN GRIDDLE CAKES

KNOWN AS AREPAS, *THESE ARE A STAPLE BREAD IN SEVERAL LATIN AMERICAN COUNTRIES, PARTICULARLY COLOMBIA AND VENEZUELA. EAT THEM FILLED WITH SOFT WHITE CHEESE, AS HERE, OR PLAIN AS AN ACCOMPANIMENT. WITH THEIR CRISP CRUST AND CHEWY INTERIOR, AREPAS CAN BECOME STALE VERY QUICKLY, SO ARE BEST EATEN PIPING HOT.*

MAKES FIFTEEN

INGREDIENTS
   200g/7oz/1¾ cups *masarepa* (or
     masa harina)
   2.5ml/½ tsp salt
   300ml/½ pint/1¼ cups water
   15ml/1 tbsp oil
   200g/7oz fresh white cheese, such
     as queso fresco or mozzarella,
     roughly chopped

1 Combine the *masarepa* or *masa harina* and salt in a bowl. Gradually stir in the water to make a soft dough, then set aside for about 20 minutes.

2 Divide the dough into 15 equal-sized balls, then, using your fingers, flatten each ball into a circle, approximately 1cm/½in thick.

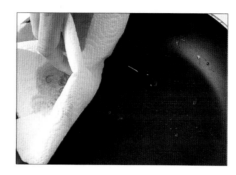

3 Heat 5ml/1 tsp of the oil in a large, heavy frying pan over a medium heat. Using a piece of kitchen paper, gently wipe the surface of the frying pan, leaving it just lightly greased.

4 Place five of the *arepas* in the frying pan. Cook for about 4 minutes, then flip over and cook for a further 4 minutes. The *arepas* should be lightly blistered on both sides.

5 Open the *arepas* and fill each with a few small pieces of fresh white cheese. Return to the pan to cook until the cheese begins to melt. Remove from the heat and keep warm.

6 Cook the remaining ten *arepas* in the same way, oiling the pan and wiping with kitchen paper between batches, to ensure it is always lightly greased. Serve the arepas while still warm so that the melted cheese is soft and runny.

COOK'S TIP
Masarepa is a flour made with the white corn grown in the Andes. Look for it in Latin American food stores. If not available, replace it with *masa harina*, the flour used to make tamales. The result will not be quite as delicate, but the *arepas* will be equally delicious.

VARIATION
Instead of cheese, try a delicious beef filling. Simply fry some minced (ground) beef in oil with ½ chopped onion, 1 small red chilli, finely chopped, 1 crushed garlic clove, ground black pepper and fresh thyme. When thoroughly cooked, stuff the mixture inside the *arepas*.

CASSAVA CHIPS

FOR A PERFECT SUNDOWNER, THERE'S NOTHING QUITE LIKE ENJOYING AN ICE-COLD BEER WITH SOME FRESHLY COOKED, GOLDEN CASSAVA CHIPS. DON'T WORRY ABOUT CUTTING PERFECT-SIZED CHIPS; THEY SHOULD BE CHUNKY AND IRREGULAR, AND EXTRA CRISP.

SERVES FOUR

INGREDIENTS
    800g/1¾lb cassava
    vegetable oil, for frying
    salt

1 Peel the cassava and cut it lengthways into 5cm/2in-wide pieces. Then cut these pieces into slices, about 2cm/¾in thick.

2 Place the slices in a large pan of salted water and bring to the boil. Lower the heat until the water simmers and cover the pan.

3 Cook the cassava for approximately 15 minutes, or until the slices are tender and just beginning to break up. Drain the cassava thoroughly and pat dry with kitchen paper.

4 Pour vegetable oil to a depth of 5cm/2in in a deep wide pan. Heat the oil, then add the cassava pieces. Fry for 3–4 minutes, turning occasionally, until the chips are golden and crisp all over. You may need to do this in batches.

5 Lift the chips from the pan with a slotted spoon and drain on kitchen paper. Season with salt and serve warm or at room temperature.

VARIATION
The chips are sometimes served with a sprinkling of grated Parmesan, in which case they will not need as much salt.

CHEESE TAMALES

CORN MEAL DUMPLINGS STEAMED IN CORN HUSKS ARE TO BE FOUND THROUGHOUT SOUTH AMERICA. THE RECIPE VARIES, WITH FRESH CORN KERNELS BEING USED INSTEAD OF CORN MEAL ON SOME OCCASIONS. THERE ARE MANY POSSIBLE FILLINGS; THIS RECIPE HAS ONE OF THE SIMPLEST.

MAKES TEN

INGREDIENTS
   10 large dried corn husks or
      greaseproof (waxed) paper
   75g/3oz/6 tbsp lard or white cooking
      fat, at room temperature
   225g/8oz/2 cups *masa harina*
   5ml/1 tsp salt
   5ml/1 tsp baking powder
   250–300ml/8–10fl oz/1–1¼ cups
      warm light vegetable stock
   200g/7oz fresh white cheese, such as
      feta, roughly chopped

1 Place the corn husks in a bowl and pour over boiling water to cover. Soak for 30 minutes, until the husks become soft and pliable. Remove from the water and pat dry with a clean dishtowel.

2 Meanwhile put the lard or white cooking fat in a mixing bowl and beat with an electric whisk until light and fluffy. Test by dropping a small amount of the whipped lard into a cup of water. If it floats, it is ready to use.

3 Combine the *masa harina*, salt and baking powder in a separate bowl. Gradually add to the lard, beating in 45ml/3 tbsp at a time. As the mixture begins to thicken, start adding the stock, alternating the dry mixture and the stock until both have been used and the mixture is light and spreadable. If it feels tough, or dry to the touch, beat in a little more warm water, but don't add more stock, as the dough will already be flavoursome enough.

4 To assemble, lay the prepared corn husks on a board and spread about one-tenth of the *masa* mixture in the centre of each, leaving a small border at either side, with a larger border at the top and bottom.

5 Place a piece of cheese in the centre of the *masa* mixture. Fold one of the longer lengths of husk over, so that it covers the filling, then repeat with the opposite end. Close the package by folding over the two remaining sides, to make a neat parcel. Secure the tamales by tying each one with a piece of string or strip of corn husk.

6 Pile the tamales in a steamer basket placed over simmering water. Cover and steam for 1 hour. Check the level of the water occasionally, topping up if necessary. The tamales are ready when the dough comes away from the corn husk cleanly. Allow to stand for 10 minutes, then serve.

COOK'S TIP
Masa harina is a flour made with finely ground dried white corn kernels. It is most famously used to make corn tortillas, to which it imparts a nutty flavour. *Masa harina* can be found in Latin food stores and markets.

TAMALES DE PICADILLO

IN ANCIENT TIMES THESE LITTLE PARCELS MADE FROM CORN HUSKS, POPULAR THROUGHOUT THE WHOLE OF MEXICO, WERE COOKED IN THE HOT ASHES OF A CAMP FIRE.

MAKES TWELVE

INGREDIENTS
    12 dried corn husks
    50g/2oz/¼ cup lard or white cooking fat
    150g/5oz/1 cup *masa harina*
    2.5ml/½ tsp salt
    5ml/1tsp baking powder
    175ml/6fl oz/¾ cup chicken stock
For the picadillo
    15ml/1 tbsp olive or corn oil
    450g/1lb minced (ground) beef
    ½ onion, finely chopped
    1 garlic clove, chopped
    1 eating apple
    225g/½lb tomatoes, peeled, seeded
      and chopped
    1 or 2 drained pickled jalapeño
      chillies, seeded and chopped
    25g/1oz raisins
    1.5ml/¼ tsp ground cinnamon
    1.5ml/¼ tsp ground cumin
    salt and ground black pepper

1 Soak the corn husks in warm water for about 30 minutes until pliable.

2 Meanwhile, make the picadillo. Heat the oil in a frying pan. Add the beef, chopped onion and garlic, and cook, stirring, until the beef is brown and the onion is tender.

3 Peel, core and chop the apple. Add the pieces to the pan with all of the remaining picadillo ingredients. Cook, uncovered, for about 20–25 minutes, stirring occasionally to prevent sticking.

4 In a bowl, cream the lard until it is light and fluffy. Mix the *masa harina* with the salt and baking powder, then gradually beat it into the lard, taking care not to add too much at once.

5 Warm the chicken stock slowly. It should not be hot or it will melt the lard.

6 Gradually beat enough of the chicken stock into the *masa* mixture to make a mushy dough. To see if the dough is ready, carefully place a small piece on top of a bowl of water. If it floats, the dough is ready; if it sinks, continue to beat the dough until the texture is light enough for it to float.

7 Drain a corn husk and lay it flat on a board. Spread about 30ml/2 tbsp of the dough down the centre part of the husk, leaving plenty of room all round for folding. Spoon 30ml/2 tbsp of the picadillo on to the centre of the dough.

8 Roll up the husk from one long side, so that the filling is completely enclosed, then fold the ends of the husks under. Make more tamales in the same way.

9 Prepare a steamer or use a metal colander and a deep pan into which the colander will fit with about 2.5cm/1in space all around.

10 Put the tamales in the steamer, folded ends under. Alternatively, place them in the colander and pour boiling water into the pan to within 2.5cm/1in of the bottom of the colander. Steam the tamales for about 1 hour, or until the dough comes away from the husk. Top up the water as required to prevent the tamales from drying.

11 Serve the tamales immediately, in the husk, leaving guests to open them at the table to reveal the delicious picadillo filling inside.

MIXED TOSTADAS

LIKE LITTLE EDIBLE PLATES, THESE TRADITIONAL MEXICAN FRIED TORTILLAS CAN SUPPORT ALMOST ANY INGREDIENTS YOU LIKE, SO LONG AS THEY ARE NOT TOO JUICY.

MAKES FOURTEEN

INGREDIENTS

  oil, for shallow frying
  14 freshly prepared unbaked
    corn tortillas
  225g/8oz/1 cup mashed red kidney
    or pinto beans
  1 iceberg lettuce, shredded
  olive oil and vinegar dressing
    (optional)
  2 cooked chicken breast portions,
    skinned and thinly sliced
  225g/8oz guacamole
  115g/4oz/1 cup coarsely grated
    mature (sharp) Cheddar cheese
  pickled jalapeño chillies, seeded and
    sliced, to taste

1 Heat the oil in a shallow frying pan and fry the corn tortillas one by one, until golden brown on both sides and crisp but not hard.

2 Spread each tortilla with a layer of mashed pinto or kidney beans. Put a layer of shredded lettuce (which can either be left plain or lightly tossed with a little dressing) over the beans.

3 Arrange chicken slices on top of the lettuce. Carefully spread over a layer of the guacamole and finally sprinkle over the grated cheese.

4 Arrange the mixed tostadas on a large platter and serve immediately, while still warm. Use your hands to eat tostadas as they are extremely messy.

VARIATIONS
• Instead of chicken, try using shredded pork, minced (ground) beef or turkey, or sliced chorizo.
• For a more authentic taste use *queso fresco* or feta cheese instead of Cheddar.

PAN-FRIED SQUID

VISIT A BEACH BAR ANYWHERE ALONG THE COAST OF SOUTH AMERICA AND THIS IS PRECISELY THE TYPE OF SNACK YOU ARE LIKELY TO FIND ON SALE.

SERVES FOUR

INGREDIENTS
1kg/2¼lb fresh small squid
30ml/2 tbsp olive oil
2 garlic cloves, crushed
1 fresh red chilli, seeded and
    finely chopped
45ml/3 tbsp *cachaça*
juice of 1 lime
salt
chunks of bread, to serve

1 Clean the squid under cold water. Pull the tentacles away from the body. The squid's entrails will come out easily. Remove the piece of cartilage from inside the body cavity and discard it.

VARIATION
If you cannot find *cachaça*, replace it with white rum or vodka.

2 Wash the body and peel away the membrane that covers it. Cut between the tentacles and head, discarding the head and entrails. Leave the tentacles whole, but discard the hard beak in the middle. Cut the body into small pieces.

3 Heat the oil over a high heat. Add the garlic, chilli and squid. Season with salt and cook for 2–3 minutes, until the squid is opaque and lightly charred.

4 Pour in the *cachaça* and continue cooking the squid until most of the liquid has evaporated. Remove the pan from the heat and then stir in the lime juice.

5 Tip the squid on to a plate and serve with chunks of bread to soak up the delicious cooking juices. Offer cocktail sticks (toothpicks) for picking up the pieces of squid.

FRIED WHITEBAIT WITH CAYENNE PEPPER

FOR THE PERFECT BEACH SNACK, TRY THESE CRISP, SPICY, BITESIZE FISH WITH A SQUEEZE OF LIME.

SERVES FOUR

INGREDIENTS
50g/2oz/½ cup plain
    (all-purpose) flour
1.5ml/¼ tsp cayenne pepper
250g/9oz whitebait
vegetable oil, for deep-frying
salt and ground black pepper
lime wedges, to serve

VARIATIONS
Small fresh anchovies are also delicious cooked whole in this way. Alternatively, make up a mixed platter using whitebait, squid and prawns (shrimp).

1 Sift the flour and cayenne pepper into a deep bowl or large shallow dish. Season with plenty of salt and ground black pepper.

2 Thoroughly coat the whitebait in the seasoned flour, then shake off any excess flour and make sure the whitebait are separate. Do this in batches, placing the coated fish on a plate ready for frying.

3 Pour oil to a depth of 5cm/2in into a deep wide pan. Heat the oil until very hot, then add a batch of whitebait and fry for 2–3 minutes until golden. Remove from the pan with a slotted spoon and drain on kitchen paper. Repeat with the remaining whitebait.

4 Pile the fried whitebait on a plate, season with salt and serve immediately with the lime wedges.

BLACK-EYED BEAN AND SHRIMP FRITTERS

THIS BRAZILIAN SNACK, LOCALLY KNOWN AS ACARAJÉ, IS FROM BAHIA, A REGION HIGHLY INFLUENCED BY ITS AFRICAN SLAVE HERITAGE. WOMEN FRY THESE PATTIES TO ORDER. THEY ARE THEN CUT OPEN AND FILLED WITH VARIOUS SAUCES, ALL DELECTABLE BUT VERY MESSY TO EAT.

MAKES TEN

INGREDIENTS
  250g/9oz/1¼ cups black-eyed
    beans (peas)
  40g/1½oz/¼ cup dried shrimp
  1 onion, roughly chopped
  palm oil and vegetable oil, for frying
  salt
  chilli oil, to serve
For the filling
  30ml/2 tbsp palm oil
  115g/4oz/⅔ cup dried shrimp
  1 large onion, thinly sliced
  2 fresh hot red chillies, seeded and
    finely chopped

1 Put the black-eyed beans in a large bowl and cover with plenty of water. Soak overnight to loosen the skins. Drain, then soak for a further 30 minutes in hot (but not boiling) water.

2 Drain the beans and tip them on to a board. Rub them between your hands to separate them from their skins. The patties will be very dry if the skins are not removed.

3 Transfer the beans to a bowl and pour over cold water to cover. The loose skins will begin to rise to the surface. Remove them with a slotted spoon and throw them away. Stir the beans to encourage more skins to float to the surface, continuing until all the skins have been removed. You'll be able to chart your progress easily, as the beans lose their distinctive "eye" when peeled. Drain.

4 Blend the dried shrimp and onion in a food processor until smooth. Add the beans and blend to a thick purée. Season with salt.

5 Mix equal quantities of palm oil and vegetable oil to a depth of about 5cm/2in in a deep pan. Form the *acarajé* mixture into 10 oval shapes. Heat the oil and fry half of the fritters for 5 minutes or until golden. Lift out with a slotted spoon and drain on kitchen paper. Between batches, skim the oil to remove any burnt bits.

6 Make the filling. Heat the oil in a frying pan. When hot, add the dried shrimp and sauté for 2–3 minutes until golden. Lift out with a slotted spoon and drain on kitchen paper. Lower the heat and stir in the onion slices. Cook for 5 minutes until soft, then add the chilli. Sauté for 1 minute and set aside.

7 Cut each fritter open lengthways and fill with the onion mixture. Add a couple of dried shrimp and drizzle with chilli oil.

BEEF EMPANADAS

YOU'LL FIND THESE PASTRY TURNOVERS THROUGHOUT LATIN AMERICA, WITH COLOMBIA'S BEING PERHAPS THE MOST FAMOUS. THEY COME WITH A VARIETY OF FILLINGS, INCLUDING BEEF, PORK, VEGETABLES AND CHEESE. WHAT BETTER WAY FOR USING UP LEFTOVERS?

MAKES TWENTY

INGREDIENTS
  225g/8oz/2 cups plain
    (all-purpose) flour
  2.5ml/½ tsp salt
  90g/3½oz/scant ½ cup cold butter,
    cut into small chunks
  juice of ½ lime
  50ml/2fl oz/¼ cup lukewarm water
  vegetable oil, for deep-frying
  chilli salsa, to serve (optional)
For the filling
  450g/1lb beef shin or leg (shank)
  60ml/4 tbsp olive oil
  1.5ml/¼ tsp ground cumin
  1 garlic clove, crushed
  10ml/2 tsp paprika
  250ml/8fl oz/1 cup light beef stock
  450g/1lb potatoes, peeled and cubed
  2 tomatoes, finely chopped
  3 spring onions (scallions),
    finely chopped
  salt and ground black pepper

1 Make the filling. Cut the beef into large chunks and chop in a food processor until finely diced, but not minced (ground). This will tenderize the meat, cutting the cooking time.

2 Heat 30ml/2 tbsp of the olive oil in a wide, heavy pan over a high heat. Add the beef chunks and sauté until golden brown. Push the beef to the side and add the cumin, crushed garlic and paprika to the pan. Reduce the heat and cook, stirring gently, for around 2 minutes, until the spices begin to release their delicious aroma.

3 Stir in the stock and bring to the boil. Cover and cook over a low heat for 30 minutes. Stir in the potatoes, tomatoes and spring onions. Cook for 15 minutes more, or until the beef and potatoes are tender. Season with salt and pepper to taste, then leave to cool.

4 Meanwhile, place the flour and salt in a food processor. Add the small chunks of butter and pulse until the mixture resembles fine breadcrumbs. Combine the lime juice and water and slowly pour into the food processor, with the motor still running. As soon as the pastry comes together, tip it on to a floured surface and gently knead to a soft dough. Shape into a ball, wrap in clear film (plastic wrap) and chill for at least 20 minutes.

5 On a floured surface roll out the pastry until it is very thin. Cut out 6cm/2½in circles, using a pastry (cookie) cutter.

6 Spoon about 7.5ml/1½ tsp of the filling into the centre of a pastry circle, then brush the edges with water. Fold the pastry over to form a half-moon, then press around the edges to seal. Repeat with the rest of the pastry.

7 Pour vegetable oil to a depth of 5cm/2in into a deep frying pan. Heat the oil, then add five or six empanadas. Fry for 5 minutes until golden brown, turning halfway through cooking. Remove from the pan with a slotted spoon and drain. Repeat with the remaining empanadas. Serve with a little chilli salsa, if using.

NUT BRITTLE

NUTS ARE VERY POPULAR IN SOUTH AMERICA AND VARIATIONS OF THIS SNACK ARE TO BE FOUND THROUGHOUT THE CONTINENT. IN BRAZIL IT'S CALLED PE-DE-MOLEQUE (KID'S FEET).

MAKES ABOUT TEN

INGREDIENTS
vegetable oil, for greasing
250g/9oz/2¼ cups unsalted peanuts
250g/9oz/generous 1 cup
   granulated sugar

COOK'S TIP
Act quickly once the sugar has reached the ideal colour, otherwise the caramel could burn and become bitter. Don't worry if the pieces of brittle don't snap evenly when cooled – they'll be just as delicious if irregular.

1 Using vegetable oil, grease a shallow 30 x 20cm/12 x 8in baking tin (pan). Tip the sugar and peanuts into a heavy pan and place over a low heat.

2 As the sugar begins to melt, start stirring the nuts with a wooden spoon, bringing the sugar that is beginning to caramelize around the edges of the pan into the centre.

3 When all the mixture has caramelized and has taken on a deep brown colour, remove the pan from the heat and quickly pour the mixture into the prepared baking tin. Leave it to cool.

4 When the brittle has almost set, use a knife to mark it into regular squares or rectangles. This will make it easier to snap the cold brittle into pieces.

COCONUT SWEETS

THESE CHEWY SWEETS (CANDIES) ARE A FAVOURITE WITH CHILDREN. THEY CAN BE MADE PLAIN, BUT THE LIME JUICE AND CLOVES ADD AN INTERESTING TWIST THAT ADULTS CANNOT RESIST EITHER.

MAKES TWENTY-FIVE

INGREDIENTS
50g/2oz/⅔ cup desiccated (dry
   unsweetened shredded) coconut
105ml/7 tbsp water
175g/6oz/¾ cup light muscovado
   (brown) sugar
large pinch ground cloves
juice of ½ lime

1 Line a baking tray with baking parchment. Place the coconut in a pan with the water and sugar. Heat gently until the sugar dissolves.

2 Stir in the ground cloves and lime juice and increase the heat. Cook, stirring with a wooden spoon, until the mixture has thickened and become dark golden brown.

3 Drop spoonfuls of the mixture on to the lined tray, pressing the mixture down with the back of the spoon to flatten it lightly into chunky, irregular pieces. Leave to cool before eating.

VARIATION
Equal quantities of grated fresh coconut and grated raw pumpkin can be used instead of the desiccated coconut.

SOUPS

The colonizers of Latin America introduced soup to the region, transforming their original recipes by using local ingredients. Light dishes, such as heart of palm soup or corn soup, are ideal as an appetizer, while heartier soups, such as chilli clam broth make excellent light meals.

CREAMY HEART OF PALM SOUP

THIS DELICATE SOUP HAS A LUXURIOUS, CREAMY, ALMOST VELVETY TEXTURE. THE SUBTLE YET DISTINCTIVE FLAVOUR OF THE PALM HEARTS IS LIKE NO OTHER, ALTHOUGH IT IS MILDLY REMINISCENT OF ARTICHOKES AND ASPARAGUS. SERVE WITH FRESH BREAD FOR A SATISFYING LUNCH.

SERVES FOUR

INGREDIENTS
  25g/1oz/2 tbsp butter
  10ml/2 tsp olive oil
  1 onion, finely chopped
  1 large leek, finely sliced
  15ml/1 tbsp plain (all-purpose) flour
  1 litre/1¾ pints/4 cups
    well-flavoured chicken stock
  350g/12oz potatoes, peeled
    and cubed
  2 x 400g/14oz cans hearts of palm,
    drained and sliced
  250ml/8fl oz/1 cup double
    (heavy) cream
  salt and ground black pepper
  cayenne pepper and chopped fresh
    chives, to garnish

1 Heat the butter and oil in a large pan over a low heat. Add the onion and leek and stir well until coated in butter. Cover and cook for 5 minutes until softened and translucent.

2 Sprinkle over the flour. Cook, stirring, for 1 minute.

3 Pour in the stock and add the potatoes. Bring to the boil, then lower the heat and simmer for 10 minutes. Stir in the hearts of palm and the cream, and simmer gently for 10 minutes.

4 Process in a blender or food processor until smooth. Return the soup to the pan and heat gently, adding a little water if necessary. The consistency should be thick but not too heavy. Season with salt and ground black pepper.

5 Ladle the soup into heated bowls and garnish each with a pinch of cayenne pepper and a scattering of fresh chives. Serve immediately.

VARIATION
For a richer, buttery flavour, add the flesh of a ripe avocado when blending.

PEANUT <u>AND</u> POTATO SOUP <u>WITH</u> CORIANDER

PEANUT SOUP IS A FIRM FAVOURITE THROUGHOUT CENTRAL AND SOUTH AMERICA, AND IS PARTICULARLY POPULAR IN BOLIVIA AND ECUADOR. AS IN MANY LATIN AMERICAN RECIPES, THE GROUND NUTS ARE USED AS A THICKENING AGENT, WITH UNEXPECTEDLY DELICIOUS RESULTS.

SERVES SIX

INGREDIENTS
   60ml/4 tbsp peanut oil
   1 onion, finely chopped
   2 garlic cloves, crushed
   1 red (bell) pepper, seeded
      and chopped
   250g/9oz potatoes, peeled and diced
   2 fresh red chillies, seeded and
      chopped
   200g/7oz canned chopped tomatoes
   150g/5oz/1¼ cups unsalted peanuts
   1.5 litres/2½ pints/6¼ cups beef stock
   salt and ground black pepper
   30ml/2 tbsp chopped fresh coriander
      (cilantro), to garnish

1 Heat the oil in a large heavy pan over a low heat. Stir in the onion and cook for 5 minutes, until beginning to soften. Add the garlic, pepper, potatoes, chillies and tomatoes. Stir well to coat the vegetables evenly in the oil, cover and cook for 5 minutes, until softened.

2 Meanwhile, toast the peanuts by gently cooking them in a large dry frying pan over a medium heat. Keep a close eye on them, moving the peanuts around the pan until they are evenly golden. Take care not to burn them.

COOK'S TIP
Replace the unsalted peanuts with peanut butter if you like. Use equal quantities of chunky and smooth peanut butter for the ideal texture.

3 Set 30ml/2 tbsp of the peanuts aside, to use as garnish. Transfer the remaining peanuts to a food processor and process until finely ground. Add the vegetables and process again until smooth.

4 Return the mixture to the pan and stir in the beef stock. Bring to the boil, then lower the heat and simmer for 10 minutes.

5 Pour the soup into heated bowls. Garnish with a generous scattering of coriander and the remaining peanuts.

CRAB, COCONUT AND CORIANDER SOUP

QUICK AND EASY TO PREPARE, THIS SOUP HAS ALL THE FLAVOURS ASSOCIATED WITH THE BAHIA REGION OF BRAZIL: CREAMY COCONUT, PALM OIL, FRAGRANT CORIANDER AND, OF COURSE, CHILLI.

SERVES FOUR

INGREDIENTS

30ml/2 tbsp olive oil

1 onion, finely chopped

1 celery stick, finely chopped

2 garlic cloves, crushed

1 fresh red chilli, seeded and chopped

1 large tomato, peeled and chopped

45ml/3 tbsp chopped fresh coriander (cilantro)

1 litre/1¾ pints/4 cups fresh crab or fish stock

500g/1¼lb crab meat

250ml/8fl oz/1 cup coconut milk

30ml/2 tbsp palm oil

juice of 1 lime

salt

hot chilli oil and lime wedges, to serve

1 Heat the olive oil in a pan over a low heat. Stir in the onion and celery, and sauté gently for 5 minutes, until softened and translucent. Stir in the garlic and chilli and cook for a further 2 minutes.

2 Add the tomato and half the coriander and increase the heat. Cook, stirring, for 3 minutes, then add the stock. Bring to the boil, then simmer for 5 minutes.

3 Stir the crab, coconut milk and palm oil into the pan and simmer over a very low heat for a further 5 minutes. The consistency should be thick, but not stew-like, so add some water if needed.

4 Stir in the lime juice and remaining coriander, then season with salt to taste. Serve in heated bowls with the chilli oil and lime wedges on the side.

CHILLI CLAM BROTH

THIS SOUP OF SUCCULENT CLAMS IN A TASTY STOCK COULD NOT BE EASIER TO PREPARE. POPULAR IN COASTAL AREAS OF COLOMBIA, IT MAKES THE PERFECT LUNCH ON A HOT SUMMER'S DAY.

SERVES SIX

INGREDIENTS
    30ml/2 tbsp olive oil
    1 onion, finely chopped
    3 garlic cloves, crushed
    2 fresh red chillies, seeded and
      finely chopped
    250ml/8fl oz/1 cup dry white wine
    400ml/14fl oz can plum tomatoes,
      drained
    1 large potato, about 250g/9oz,
      peeled and diced
    400ml/14fl oz/1⅔ cups fish stock
    1.3kg/3lb fresh clams
    15ml/1 tbsp chopped fresh
      coriander (cilantro)
    15ml/1 tbsp chopped fresh flat
      leaf parsley
    salt
    lime wedges, to garnish

1 Heat the oil in a pan. Add the onion and sauté for 5 minutes over a low heat. Stir in the garlic and chillies and cook for a further 2 minutes. Pour in the wine and bring to the boil, then simmer for 2 minutes.

2 Add the tomatoes, diced potato and stock. Bring to the boil, cover and lower the heat so that the soup simmers.

3 Season with salt and cook for 15 minutes, until the potatoes are beginning to break up and the tomatoes have made a rich sauce.

4 Meanwhile, wash the clams thoroughly under cold running water. Gently tap any that are open, and discard them if they do not close.

5 Add the clams to the soup, cover the pan and cook for about 3–4 minutes, or until the clams have opened, then stir in the chopped herbs. Season with salt to taste.

6 Check over the clams and throw away any that have failed to open. Ladle the soup into warmed bowls. Offer the lime wedges separately, to be squeezed over the soup just before eating.

CHUNKY PRAWN CHUPE

CHOWDERS, KNOWN AS CHUPES IN SOUTH AMERICA, ARE A MEAL IN THEMSELVES. POTATOES ARE ALWAYS INCLUDED, BUT THE OTHER INGREDIENTS VARY. THIS IS A SEAFOOD VERSION.

SERVES SIX

INGREDIENTS
  500g/1¼lb raw king prawns
    (jumbo shrimp)
  750ml/1¼ pints/3 cups fish stock
  1 carrot, finely chopped
  2 celery sticks, thinly sliced
  45ml/3 tbsp annatto (achiote) oil
  1 large onion, finely chopped
  1 red (bell) pepper, seeded and diced
  2 garlic cloves, crushed
  2 fresh red chillies, seeded
    and chopped
  5ml/1 tsp turmeric
  1 large tomato, peeled and chopped
  675g/1½lb potatoes, peeled and cut
    into 2.5cm/1in cubes
  115g/4oz/1 cup fresh or frozen peas
  15ml/1 tbsp chopped fresh mint
  15ml/1 tbsp chopped fresh
    coriander (cilantro)
  salt

1 Peel the prawns and set them aside. Place the shells in a large pan with the fish stock, carrot and celery. Bring to the boil, then simmer over a low heat for 20 minutes. Strain into a bowl or jug (pitcher) and set the stock aside.

VARIATION
Traditionally this soup would be made using *huacatay*, a pungent Peruvian herb that tastes like a cross between mint and coriander (cilantro).

2 Heat the oil in a large pan over a low heat. Stir in the onion and red pepper and sauté for 5 minutes. Stir in the garlic, chillies and turmeric and cook for a further 2 minutes.

3 Add the chopped tomato and potatoes to the pan, season to taste with salt and cook for about 10 minutes, allowing the tomato to break down slightly and the potatoes to absorb the flavours of the other ingredients.

4 Pour in the strained stock and bring to the boil. Lower the heat and simmer for 15 minutes, or until the potatoes are cooked through.

5 Stir the prawns and peas into the soup and simmer for 4–5 minutes, or until the prawns become opaque. Finally, stir in the mint and coriander, and serve in warmed bowls.

CORN SOUP

CORN SOUP TURNS UP ALL OVER LATIN AMERICA. TOMATOES ARE OFTEN COOKED WITH THE ONION, BUT HERE THEY ARE SPRINKLED OVER THE SOUP, LEAVING THE FLAVOURS FRESH AND DISTINCT.

SERVES FOUR

INGREDIENTS
  40g/1½oz/3 tbsp butter
  1 large onion, finely chopped
  500g/1¼lb fresh or thawed frozen
    corn kernels
  1 litre/1¾ pints/4 cups chicken stock
  250ml/8fl oz/1 cup double
    (heavy) cream
  salt and ground black pepper
  1 tomato, peeled, seeded and
    chopped, to garnish

VARIATION
The corn kernels make this soup very sweet. If it is not to your taste, add 350g/12oz diced potato to the pan at the same time as the corn. Increase the chicken stock accordingly.

1 Melt the butter in a large heavy pan. Stir in the onion and cook over a low heat for 5 minutes or until softened and translucent.

2 Add the corn and the stock, increase the heat and bring to the boil. Lower the heat, cover and simmer for 10 minutes, until the corn is tender.

3 Pour the soup into a blender or food processor and process until smooth. Return to the pan and stir in the cream. Bring to the boil, then season with salt and pepper to taste.

4 Ladle the soup into heated bowls, garnish with the chopped tomato and serve immediately.

FISH AND SHELLFISH

Fish and shellfish play an important part in Latin-American cuisine — and the most popular recipes rely on the freshest fish cooked simply. In parts of Brazil, where the local cuisine has been shaped by African slave influences, richly flavoured fish and shellfish stews are more popular.

BAKED SEA BASS WITH COCONUT

THIS ELEGANT COLOMBIAN DISH IS IDEAL FOR A DINNER PARTY. THE BAY LEAVES GIVE A DEPTH OF FLAVOUR TO THE CHILLI AND COCONUT SAUCE.

SERVES FOUR

INGREDIENTS

   1 whole large sea bass, about
      900g/2lb, cleaned
   2 fresh red chillies, seeded and
      finely chopped
   1 onion, finely sliced
   2 garlic cloves, crushed
   juice of 1 lime
   15ml/1 tbsp olive oil
   2 bay leaves
   200ml/7fl oz/scant 1 cup
      coconut milk
   salt

VARIATION
For a complete meal, cook some vegetables in the roasting pan with the sea bass. Sliced carrots, fennel or/and courgettes (zucchini) would all go well with the coconut sauce.

1 Preheat the oven to 180°C/350°F/ Gas 4. Thoroughly rinse the fish inside and out, then pat dry with kitchen paper. Place in a large roasting pan and season all over with salt.

2 Generously sprinkle the chopped chillies, onion, garlic, lime juice and olive oil over the fish. Add the bay leaves to the pan and bake the fish in the oven for about 15 minutes.

3 Pour the coconut milk over the fish and return it to the oven for a further 10 minutes, or until the flesh flakes easily when tested with the tip of a sharp knife.

4 Cut along the back of the fish. This will release the flesh from the bones, making it easy to divide into portions. Serve with the sauce. A rice dish would make a good accompaniment.

PAN-FRIED SEA BREAM WITH LIME AND TOMATO SALSA

THE MOST POPULAR WAY OF COOKING A FRESH PIECE OF FISH IS TO PAN FRY IT OR GRILL IT. IN THIS RECIPE A SIMPLE SALSA IS FLASHED IN THE PAN AT THE END OF COOKING, TO MAKE A LIGHT SAUCE.

SERVES FOUR

INGREDIENTS

   4 sea bream fillets
   juice of 2 limes
   30ml/2 tbsp chopped coriander
      (cilantro)
   1 fresh red chilli, seeded and
      finely chopped
   2 spring onions (scallions), sliced
   45ml/3 tbsp olive oil, plus extra
      to serve
   2 large tomatoes, diced
   salt
   cooked white rice, to serve

1 Place the fish fillets in a shallow china or glass dish large enough to hold them all in a single layer.

2 Mix the lime juice, coriander, chilli and spring onions in a jug (pitcher). Stir in half the oil, then pour this marinade over the fish. Cover and marinate for around 15–20 minutes. Do not be tempted to marinate the fish for longer than this or the acid in the marinade will start to "cook" it.

3 Heat the remaining oil in a large heavy frying pan over a high heat. Lift each piece of fish from the marinade and pat dry with kitchen paper.

4 Season the fish with salt and place in the hot pan, skin side down. Cook for 2 minutes, then turn and cook for a further 2 minutes, until the flesh is opaque all the way through.

5 Add the marinade and the chopped tomatoes to the pan. Bring the sauce to the boil and cook for about 1 minute, until the tomatoes are lightly cooked but still retain their shape. Drizzle a little olive oil over the fish and serve on individual warm plates, with white rice and the tomato salsa.

HALIBUT WITH PEPPERS AND COCONUT MILK

THIS AROMATIC DISH, KNOWN LOCALLY AS MOQUECA COMES FROM THE STATE OF BAHIA, ON THE EAST COAST OF BRAZIL. COOKED AND SERVED IN AN EARTHENWARE DISH, IT IS USUALLY ACCOMPANIED BY WHITE RICE AND FLAVOURED CASSAVA FLOUR TO SOAK UP THE DELICIOUS SAUCE.

SERVES SIX

INGREDIENTS
  6 halibut, cod, haddock or monkfish
    fillets, each about 115g/4oz
  juice of 2 limes
  8 fresh coriander (cilantro) sprigs
  2 fresh red chillies, seeded
    and chopped
  3 tomatoes, sliced into thin rounds
  1 red (bell) pepper, seeded and
    sliced into thin rounds
  1 green (bell) pepper, seeded and
    sliced into thin rounds
  1 small onion, sliced into thin rounds
  200ml/7fl oz/scant 1 cup
    coconut milk
  60ml/4 tbsp palm oil
  salt
  cooked white rice, to serve
For the flavoured cassava flour
  30ml/2 tbsp palm oil
  1 medium onion, thinly sliced
  250g/9oz/2¼ cups cassava flour

1 Place the fish fillets in a large, shallow dish and pour over water to cover. Pour in the lime juice and set aside for 30 minutes. Drain the fish thoroughly and pat dry with kitchen paper. Arrange the fish in a single layer in a heavy pan which has a tight-fitting lid.

2 Sprinkle the coriander and chillies over the fish, then top with a layer each of tomatoes, peppers and onion. Pour the coconut milk over, cover and leave to stand for 15 minutes before cooking.

3 Season with salt, then place the pan over a high heat and cook until the coconut milk comes to the boil. Lower the heat and simmer for 5 minutes. Remove the lid, pour in the palm oil, cover again and simmer for 10 minutes.

4 Meanwhile make the flavoured cassava flour. Heat the oil in a large frying pan over a very low heat. Stir in the onion slices and cook for 8–10 minutes until soft and golden. Stir in the cassava flour and cook, stirring constantly, for 1–2 minutes until lightly toasted and evenly coloured by the oil. Season with salt.

5 Serve the *moqueca* with the rice and flavoured cassava flour.

PRAWN AND POTATO OMELETTE

MORE LIKE A SPANISH TORTILLA THAN A FRENCH OMELETTE, THIS DISH MAKES A DELICIOUS LUNCH WHEN SERVED WITH A FRESH LEAFY GREEN SALAD. THE SWEET PRAWNS ARE COOKED GENTLY INSIDE THE OMELETTE, STAYING TENDER AND SUCCULENT.

SERVES SIX

INGREDIENTS

    200g/7oz potatoes, peeled and diced
    30ml/2 tbsp olive oil
    1 onion, finely sliced
    2.5ml/½ tsp paprika
    2 large tomatoes, peeled, seeded
      and chopped
    200g/7oz peeled raw prawns (shrimp)
    6 eggs
    2.5ml/½ tsp baking powder
    salt

1 Cook the potatoes in a pan of salted boiling water for about 10 minutes or until tender.

2 Meanwhile, pour the oil into a 23cm/9in frying pan which can safely be used under the grill (broiler). Place over a medium heat. Add the onion slices and stir well to coat evenly in the oil. Cook for 5 minutes until the onions begin to soften. Sprinkle over the paprika and cook for 1 minute more.

3 Stir in the tomatoes. Drain the cooked potatoes thoroughly and add them to the pan. Stir gently to mix. Increase the heat and cook for 10 minutes, or until the mixture has thickened and the potatoes have absorbed the flavour of the tomatoes. Remove from the heat and stir in the prawns.

4 Preheat the grill. Beat the eggs, stir in the baking powder and salt. Pour into the pan and mix thoroughly. Cover and cook for 8–10 minutes until the omelette has almost set, then finish under the grill.

SEA BASS CEVICHE

THIS TASTY DISH, ALSO KNOWN AS SEVICHE, IS PARTICULARLY POPULAR IN PERU, WHERE IT IS MADE WITH A VARIETY OF FISH AND SHELLFISH. THE RAW FISH SIMPLY "COOKS" IN A FRESH CITRUS MARINADE, AND NEEDS NO HEATING, SO IT IS VITAL THAT THE FISH IS PERFECTLY FRESH.

SERVES FOUR

INGREDIENTS

675g/1½lb sea bass fillets
300ml/½ pint/1¼ cups lime juice
200ml/7oz orange juice
2 fresh red chillies, seeded and
  finely sliced
1 medium red onion, finely sliced
30ml/2 tbsp fresh coriander
  (cilantro) leaves
1 large tomato, seeded and chopped
salt and ground black pepper
green salad and crusty bread,
  to serve

1 Cut the sea bass fillets into 2.5cm/1in strips, removing any stray bones with tweezers. Place the fish in a bowl and season with salt and pepper.

2 Pour the lime juice and orange juice over the fish, then gently stir in the chillies and onion slices. The fish must be totally immersed in the marinade, so add a little more juice if necessary.

3 Cover with clear film (plastic wrap) and chill for at least 2 hours, until the fish becomes opaque.

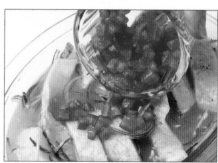

4 Stir the coriander leaves and chopped tomato into the ceviche and serve with a green salad and crusty bread.

COOK'S TIP

The ceviche should be kept covered in the refrigerator right up until it is to be served. It must be eaten on the day it is made.

MACKEREL ESCABECHE

THIS TRADITIONAL WAY OF PRESERVING FISH IN VINEGAR, WAS BROUGHT TO LATIN AMERICA BY THE SPANISH AND PORTUGUESE. OILY FISH, SUCH AS MACKEREL AND SARDINES, LEND THEMSELVES PARTICULARLY WELL TO THIS TREATMENT. IT TAKES AT LEAST A DAY, SO ALLOW PLENTY OF TIME.

SERVES SIX

INGREDIENTS

12 small mackerel fillets
juice of 2 limes
90ml/6 tbsp olive oil
2 red onions, thinly sliced
2 garlic cloves, thinly sliced
2 bay leaves
6 black peppercorns
120ml/4fl oz/½ cup red wine vinegar
50g/2oz/½ cup plain
    (all-purpose) flour
salt and ground black pepper

1 Place the mackerel fillets side by side in a large, shallow glass or china dish. Pour over the lime juice. Season with salt and pepper and cover. Marinate in the refrigerator for 20–30 minutes, but no longer.

2 Meanwhile, heat half the oil in a frying pan. Add the onions and cook over a low heat for 10 minutes, until softened but not coloured. Stir in the garlic and cook for 2 minutes.

3 Add the bay leaves, peppercorns and vinegar to the pan and simmer over a very low heat for 5 minutes.

COOK'S TIP

If you are planning to keep the fish for more than one day, make sure it is completely immersed in the vinegar, then top with a thin layer of olive oil. Cover tightly. It will keep in the refrigerator for up to 1 month.

4 Pat the mackerel fillets dry and coat them in the flour. Heat the remaining oil in a large frying pan and fry the fish, in batches, for 2 minutes on each side.

5 Return the fish to the dish in which they were originally marinated. Pour the vinegar marinade over the fish. Leave to marinate for 24 hours before serving.

MARINATED RED MULLET

This popular Latin American recipe is based on a Spanish way of cooking fish en escabeche by first frying it, then marinating it. If you are unable to find fresh mullet, snapper, sea bream or tilapia are all good alternatives.

SERVES SIX

INGREDIENTS

7.5ml/1½ tsp mild Spanish paprika,
  preferably Spanish smoked
  pimentón
45ml/3 tbsp plain (all-purpose) flour
120ml/4fl oz/½ cup olive oil
6 red mullet, each weighing about
  300g/11oz, filleted
2 aubergines (eggplants), sliced or
  cut into long wedges
2 red or yellow (bell) peppers, seeded
  and thickly sliced
1 large red onion, thinly sliced
2 garlic cloves, sliced
15ml/1 tbsp sherry vinegar
juice of 1 lemon
brown sugar, to taste
15ml/1 tbsp chopped fresh oregano
18–24 black olives
45ml/3 tbsp chopped fresh flat
  leaf parsley
salt and ground black pepper

1 Mix 5ml/1 tsp of the paprika with the flour and season well with salt and black pepper. Heat half the oil in a large frying pan. Dip the fish into the flour, turning to coat both sides, and fry for 4–5 minutes, until browned on each side. Place the fish in a glass or china dish suitable for marinating it.

2 Add 30ml/2 tbsp of the remaining oil to the pan and fry the aubergine wedges until softened and browned. Drain thoroughly on a piece of kitchen paper to remove excess oil, then add the aubergine to the fish.

3 Add another 30ml/2 tbsp oil to the pan and cook the peppers and onion gently for 6–8 minutes, until softened but not browned. Add the garlic and remaining paprika, then cook for a further 2 minutes. Stir in the sherry vinegar and lemon juice with 30ml/2 tbsp water and heat until simmering. Season to taste with a pinch of sugar.

4 Stir in the oregano and olives, then spoon over the fish. Set aside to cool, then cover and marinate in the fridge for several hours or overnight.

5 About 30 minutes before serving, bring the fish and vegetables back to room temperature. Stir in the parsley just before serving.

COD CARAMBA

THIS COLOURFUL MEXICAN DISH, WITH ITS CONTRASTING CRUNCHY TOPPING AND TENDER FISH FILLING, CAN BE MADE WITH ANY ECONOMICAL WHITE FISH SUCH AS COLEY OR HADDOCK. SERVE WITH A TASTY GREEN SALAD FOR A HEARTY MIDWEEK SUPPER.

SERVES SIX

INGREDIENTS
  450g/1lb cod fillets
  225g/8oz smoked cod fillets
  300ml/½ pint/1¼ cups fish stock
  50g/2oz/¼ cup butter
  1 onion, sliced
  2 garlic cloves, crushed
  1 green and 1 red (bell) pepper,
    seeded and diced
  2 courgettes (zucchini), diced
  115g/4oz/⅔ cup drained canned or
    thawed frozen corn kernels
  2 tomatoes, peeled and chopped
  juice of 1 lime
  Tabasco sauce
  salt, ground black pepper and
    cayenne pepper
For the topping
  75g/3oz tortilla chips
  50g/2oz/½ cup grated Cheddar cheese
  coriander (cilantro) sprigs, to garnish
  lime wedges, to serve

1 Lay the fish in a shallow pan and pour over the fish stock. Bring to the boil, lower the heat, cover and poach for about 8 minutes, until the flesh flakes easily. Leave to cool slightly, then remove the skin and separate the flesh into large flakes. Keep hot.

2 Melt the butter in a pan, add the onion and garlic and cook gently over a low heat until soft and translucent. Add the peppers, stir and cook for about 2 minutes. Stir in the courgettes and cook for 3 minutes more, until all the vegetables are tender.

3 Stir in the corn and tomatoes, then add lime juice and Tabasco to taste. Season with salt, black pepper and cayenne. Cook for 2 minutes to heat the corn and tomatoes, then stir in the fish and transfer to a dish that can safely be used under the grill (broiler).

4 Preheat the grill. Make the topping by crushing the tortilla chips, then mixing in the grated cheese. Add cayenne pepper to taste and sprinkle over the fish. Place the dish under the grill until the topping is crisp and brown. Garnish with coriander sprigs and lime wedges.

KING PRAWNS IN A COCONUT AND NUT CREAM

FOR THIS BRAZILIAN RECIPE, COCONUT MILK IS USED TO MAKE VATAPÁ, *A LUXURIOUS SAUCE THICKENED WITH CASHEWS, PEANUTS AND BREADCRUMBS, THEN USED TO COOK PRAWNS.*

4 Grind the peanuts and cashew nuts in a food processor until they become a fine powder. Stir into the pan and cook for about 1 minute more.

SERVES SIX

INGREDIENTS
   130g/4½oz/2¼ cups fresh white
     breadcrumbs
   105ml/7 tbsp coconut milk
   30 raw king prawns (jumbo shrimp),
     about 900g/2lb
   400ml/14fl oz/1⅔ cups fish stock
   2 large tomatoes, roughly chopped
   1 onion, quartered
   2 fresh red chillies, seeded and
     roughly chopped
   130g/4½oz dried shrimps
   45ml/3 tbsp palm oil
   2 garlic cloves, crushed
   25g/1oz fresh root ginger, grated
   75g/3oz/¾ cup roasted peanuts
   50g/2oz/½ cup cashew nuts
   60ml/4 tbsp coconut cream
   juice of 1 lime
   salt and ground black pepper
   chopped fresh coriander (cilantro)
     and hot chilli oil, to serve

1 Place the breadcrumbs in a bowl and stir in the coconut milk. Leave to soak for at least 30 minutes. Purée, in a blender or food processor, then scrape into a bowl and set aside.

2 Meanwhile, peel the fresh prawns and set them aside in a cool place. Place the shells in a pan and add the fish stock and tomatoes. Bring to the boil, then simmer over a low heat for 30 minutes. Strain into a bowl, pressing the prawn shells against the sides of the sieve with a wooden spoon to extract as much flavour as possible. Reserve the prawn stock but discard the shells.

3 Put the onion, chillies and dried shrimps in a blender or food processor and blend to a purée. Scrape into a large pan and stir in the palm oil. Cook over a very low heat for 5 minutes. Add the garlic and ginger and cook for a further 2 minutes.

5 Stir in the breadcrumb purée and prawn stock and bring to the boil. Reduce the heat and continue to cook, stirring constantly, for 6–8 minutes, until thick and smooth.

6 Add the coconut cream, lime juice and prawns. Stir over the heat for 3 minutes until the prawns are cooked through and the *vatapá* resembles a thin porridge. If necessary, stir in a little water. Season with salt and black pepper.

7 Serve immediately, adding a scattering of chopped coriander and a couple of drops of chilli oil to each portion. Cooked white rice makes a good accompaniment.

VARIATIONS
• Instead of prawns, try using white fish.
• For chicken *vatapá*, replace the prawns with chicken pieces, seasoned and pan-fried in a little olive oil until tender. Use chicken stock rather than fish stock.

STUFFED CRAB

SERVE THIS SIMPLE DISH AS AN APPETIZER FOR A DINNER PARTY. A TRADITIONAL BRAZILIAN RECIPE,
IT IS USUALLY SERVED EITHER IN CRAB SHELLS OR SMALL EARTHENWARE DISHES.

SERVES SIX

INGREDIENTS
  400g/14oz crab meat
  juice of 1 lime
  50g/2oz/1 cup fresh breadcrumbs
  105ml/7 tbsp full-fat (whole) milk
  25g/1oz/2 tbsp butter
  1 onion, finely chopped
  2 garlic cloves, crushed
  2 tomatoes, finely chopped
  15ml/1 tbsp chopped fresh flat
    leaf parsley
  2 egg yolks, plus extra for glazing
  15ml/1 tbsp dried breadcrumbs
  15ml/1 tbsp grated Parmesan cheese
  salt
  lemon wedges, to serve

1 Place the crab meat in a large glass bowl and squeeze over the lime juice. Marinate for about 20 minutes. Meanwhile, put the breadcrumbs in a separate bowl with the milk and leave to soak for 10 minutes.

2 Melt the butter in a pan over a low heat. Add the chopped onion and cook gently for 10 minutes until softened. Stir in the crushed garlic and cook for 1 minute more. Drain the crab meat and squeeze out all of the excess liquid from the breadcrumbs.

COOK'S TIP
The crab mixture can be prepared in advance. Spoon it into the individual crab shells or bowls and cover. Keep refrigerated until needed, then add the topping and bake in a preheated oven at 200°C/400°F/Gas 6 for 10–15 minutes.

3 Add the crab meat, tomatoes and breadcrumbs to the pan and stir well to combine. Return to a medium heat and cook, stirring, for 4–5 minutes. Stir in the chopped parsley and season to taste with salt and ground pepper – the mixture should actually taste over-seasoned at this stage.

4 Lower the heat and add the egg yolks, stirring vigorously for 1 minute. Do not allow the mixture to boil.

5 Preheat the grill (broiler). Transfer the mixture to six empty crab shells, or small ovenproof dishes and brush with beaten egg yolk. Combine the dried breadcrumbs and Parmesan and sprinkle a thin coating over the crab meat. Grill (broil) for 3–4 minutes, until golden. Serve with the lemon wedges.

CHILEAN SQUID CASSEROLE

THIS HEARTY STEW IS IDEAL ON A COLD EVENING. THE POTATOES DISINTEGRATE TO THICKEN AND ENRICH THE SAUCE, MAKING A WARMING, COMFORTING MAIN COURSE.

SERVES SIX

INGREDIENTS

800g/1¾lb squid
45ml/3 tbsp olive oil
5 garlic cloves, crushed
4 fresh jalapeño chillies, seeded and
  finely chopped
2 celery sticks, diced
500g/1¼lb small new potatoes or
  baby salad potatoes, scrubbed,
  scraped or peeled and quartered
400ml/14fl oz/1⅔ cups dry
  white wine
400ml/14fl oz/1⅔ cups fish stock
4 tomatoes, diced
30ml/2 tbsp chopped fresh flat
  leaf parsley
salt
white rice or *arepas* (corn breads),
  to serve

1 Clean the squid under cold water. Pull the tentacles away from the body. The squid's entrails will come out easily. Remove the cartilage from inside the body cavity and discard it. Wash the body thoroughly.

2 Pull away the membrane that covers the body. Cut between the tentacles and head, discarding the head and entrails. Leave the tentacles whole but discard the hard beak in the middle. Cut the body into thin rounds.

COOK'S TIP
Adding the tomatoes and parsley at the end gives a real freshness to the sauce. If you'd prefer an even heartier dish, add these ingredients to the pan with the potatoes. Replace the white wine with a Chilean cabernet sauvignon.

3 Heat the oil, add the garlic, chillies and celery and cook for 5 minutes. Stir in the potatoes, then add the wine and stock. Bring to the boil, then simmer, covered, for 25 minutes.

4 Remove from the heat and stir in the squid, tomatoes and parsley. Cover the pan and leave to stand until the squid is cooked. Serve immediately.

CHILEAN SEAFOOD PLATTER

FRESHNESS IS IMPORTANT FOR THIS RAW SEAFOOD APPETIZER, SO CHILEAN COOKS USE THE PRIME CATCH OF THE DAY, INCLUDING EXOTIC SHELLFISH. YOU CAN USE WHATEVER IS AVAILABLE LOCALLY.

SERVES SIX

INGREDIENTS
  450g/1lb raw king prawns
    (jumbo shrimp)
  12 clams
  12 mussels
  6 scallops
  6 oysters
  12 razor clams
  lime wedges, to serve
For the salsa
  60ml/4 tbsp chopped fresh
    coriander (cilantro)
  15ml/1 tbsp chopped fresh flat
    leaf parsley
  2 shallots, finely chopped
  1 fresh green chilli, seeded and
    finely chopped
  juice of 2 limes
  30ml/2 tbsp olive oil
  salt

3 Use an oyster knife to open the raw shellfish. Push the point of the knife into the hinge, then twist to loosen. Push the knife along the edge of the whole shell so it can be opened.

4 Use the knife to loosen the fish from their shells and carefully remove the black "string" that runs along the edge of the scallop.

5 Arrange the seafood, in the shells, on a platter and serve with the fresh coriander and chilli salsa, and lime wedges, if you like. Eat immediately.

1 Combine the salsa ingredients in a bowl and season to taste. Make the salsa a few hours in advance, if possible, so that the delicate flavours have time to develop.

2 Bring a pan of salted water to the boil. Plunge the prawns into the water and remove from the pan as soon as they turn pink. Refresh the prawns in a bowl of cold water, drain and set aside.

COOK'S TIP
If you prefer to cook the shellfish, it could be steamed quickly and then refreshed in cold water before being served. Do not overcook the shellfish, or it will become tough.

MEAT

The gaucho nations of Argentina, Paraguay and Uruguay are real meat-eaters, and large cuts of beef, lamb and pork are cooked whole at their famous barbecues. Richly flavoured stews and pot roasts are also popular, made with herbs, spices and fruits, as is a combination of mixed meats, such as the Brazilian national dish Feijoada.

THE GAUCHO BARBECUE

THERE IS NO BETTER WAY OF ENJOYING THE PRESTIGIOUS PAMPAS BEEF THAN WITH A TRADITIONAL BARBECUE. THE MEAT IS COOKED SIMPLY, WITH NO NEED FOR RUBS OR MARINADES, THEN ENJOYED WITH A DELICIOUS SELECTION OF SALADS AND SALSAS.

SERVES SIX

INGREDIENTS

   50g/2oz/¼ cup coarse sea salt
   200ml/7fl oz/ scant 1 cup
    warm water
   6 pork sausages
   1kg/2¼lb beef short ribs
   1kg/2¼lb rump (round) steak, in
    one piece
   salads, salsas and breads, to serve

COOK'S TIP
Regularly basting the meat in salted water keeps it moist and succulent.

1 Dissolve the sea salt in the warm water in a bowl. Leave to cool.

2 Prepare the barbecue. If you are using a charcoal grill, light the coals about 40 minutes before you want to start cooking. Wait until the coals are no longer red but are covered in white ash. Occasionally add coals to the barbecue to maintain this temperature.

3 Start by cooking the sausages, which should take 15–20 minutes depending on the size. Once cooked on all sides, slice the sausages thickly and arrange on a plate. Let guests help themselves while you cook the remaining meats.

4 The short ribs should be placed bony side down on the grill. Cook for 15 minutes, turn, brush the cooked side of each rib with brine and grill for a further 25–30 minutes. Slice and transfer to a plate for guests to help themselves.

5 Place the whole rump steak on the grill and cook for 5 minutes, then turn over and baste the browned side with brine. Continue turning and basting in this way for 20–25 minutes in total, until the meat is cooked to your liking. Allow the meat to rest for 5 minutes, then slice thinly and serve with salads, salsa and bread.

VARIATION
A selection of meat cuts can be used, from sirloin to flank steak or chuck steak. Sweetbreads, skewered chicken hearts and kidneys are popular additions to the Gaucho barbecue, as well as chicken, lamb and pork. The star of the show, however, will always be the beef.

BEEF STUFFED WITH EGGS AND SPINACH

THIS TRADITIONAL ARGENTINIAN DISH MAKES A GREAT LUNCH WHEN SERVED COLD WITH A SALAD, BUT CAN ALSO BE SERVED HOT FOR DINNER WITH SOME BOILED POTATOES. ITS NAME, MATAMBRE ("KILL HUNGER") IS SOMEWHAT UNFAIR; FOR ALTHOUGH FILLING, IT IS NOT A HEAVY DISH.

SERVES SIX

INGREDIENTS
   60ml/4 tbsp olive oil
   1 small carrot, finely chopped
   1 celery stick, finely chopped
   1 onion, finely chopped
   2 eggs
   675g/1½lb flank steak
   250g/9oz spinach, trimmed
   2.5ml/½ tsp cayenne pepper
   1.5 litres/2½ pints/6¼ cups beef stock
   salt and ground black pepper
   boiled potatoes or salad, to serve

1 Heat half the olive oil in a frying pan over a medium heat. Add the carrot, celery and onion and sauté for 5 minutes, until soft and beginning to colour.

2 Meanwhile hard boil the eggs. Place them in a pan with cold water to cover. Bring to the boil, then lower the heat to a simmer. Cook for 10 minutes then lift out and cool in a bowl of cold water. Shell the eggs, then slice them thinly.

3 Season the steak generously with salt and ground black pepper. Spread the cooked onion mixture over the beef, leaving a 1cm/½in border round the edge. Arrange the spinach over the onion, then top with the egg. Season with extra salt and cayenne pepper.

COOK'S TIP
Flank steak is ideal for slow cooking, becoming so tender you can almost cut it with a fork. If you cannot get flank, skirt steak is very similar.

4 Roll the meat up tightly, being careful not to lose any of the stuffing. Tie with string four or five times along the length of the roll.

5 Heat the remaining oil in a pan. Add the beef roll to the pan and cook on all sides until golden brown. Pour in the stock, then bring to the boil. Lower the heat, cover and simmer gently for 1½–2 hours, until very tender.

6 Remove the beef from the stock and slice it as thinly as possible. Serve hot with boiled potatoes or as part of a buffet or picnic.

FEIJOADA

This mixed meat and black bean stew is indisputably the national dish of Brazil and is traditionally served for Saturday lunch. It's impossible to make a good feijoada for fewer than ten people, since there are so many different types of meat involved. The meats can vary, but the beans have to be very small and black.

SERVES TWELVE

INGREDIENTS

1kg/2¼lb/5½ cups black
  turtle beans
1 smoked pig's tongue, optional
500g/1¼lb *carne seca* or beef jerky
250g/9oz salted pork ribs
350g/12oz smoked streaky (fatty)
  bacon, in one piece
500g/1¼lb smoked pork ribs
300g/11oz pork sausages
300g/11oz smoked chorizo
2 fresh bay leaves
60ml/4 tbsp vegetable oil
5 garlic cloves, crushed
salt
fresh orange slices, peeled, to serve
cooked white rice
toasted cassava flour
stir-fried kale
chilli oil

1 Wash the beans in running water, then place in a bowl with cold water to cover. Soak overnight. Rinse the tongue, *carne seca* or beef jerky, and salted pork ribs in cold running water and place in a separate bowl. Pour over water to cover and soak for 8 hours, or overnight, changing the soaking water three or four times.

2 Drain the beans and place them in a very large heavy pan. Pour in enough water to cover, and bring to the boil over a high heat. Skim the surface, then lower the heat. Cover the pan and simmer for 1 hour.

3 Meanwhile, drain the soaked meats, rinse them again under cold running water and transfer to a second large heavy pan. Add the streaky bacon and smoked pork ribs, then cover with water. Bring to the boil over a high heat, skim the surface, then cover the pan. Lower the heat and simmer for 1 hour.

4 Transfer the cooked meats, with their cooking liquid, to the pan with the beans. Add the pork sausages, chorizo and bay leaves. If necessary, add more water to cover. Bring to the boil, skim the surface, cover, and continue simmering for about 30 minutes.

5 Heat the oil in a large frying pan over a low heat. Add the crushed garlic cloves and cook, stirring, for about 2 minutes, being careful not to let it burn.

6 Ladle some beans from the large pan into the frying pan and fry, mashing the beans with a wooden spoon. Return the mashed beans to the meat mixture and lower the heat for 5 minutes. Taste the stew and add some salt if needed.

7 Lift the meats from the pan and cut them into even-size pieces. Arrange on a platter, keeping each type of meat separate. Spoon a ladleful of beans over the meats. Pour the remaining beans into a large serving bowl.

8 Take the beans and meats to the table with a platter of peeled, sliced oranges, cooked white rice, toasted cassava flour, stir-fried kale and chilli oil.

COOK'S TIPS

• *Carne seca*, a Brazilian beef jerky, can be bought in Brazilian or Portuguese food stores. You can make a *feijoada* without it, but it won't be as rich.
• Toasted cassava flour is sold in Latin American or Portuguese food stores. Here it is served from the packet, but it can be flavoured with palm oil or eggs.

BLACK BEAN CHILLI CON CARNE

FRESH GREEN AND DRIED RED CHILLIES ADD PLENTY OF FIRE TO THIS CLASSIC TEX-MEX DISH OF
TENDER BEEF COOKED IN A RICH AND SPICY TOMATO SAUCE.

SERVES SIX

INGREDIENTS

225g/8oz/1¼ cups dried black beans
500g/1¼ lb braising steak
30ml/2 tbsp vegetable oil
2 onions, chopped
1 garlic clove, crushed
1 fresh green chilli, seeded and
  finely chopped
15ml/1 tbsp paprika
10ml/2 tsp ground cumin
10ml/2 tsp ground coriander
400g/14oz can chopped tomatoes
300ml/½ pint/1¼ cups beef stock
1 dried red chilli, crumbled
5ml/1 tsp hot pepper sauce
1 fresh red (bell) pepper, seeded and
  chopped
salt
fresh coriander (cilantro), to garnish
boiled rice, to serve

1 Put the beans in a large pan. Cover with cold water, bring to the boil and boil vigorously for about 10 minutes. Drain, tip into a bowl, cover with cold water and leave to soak overnight.

2 Preheat the oven to 150°C/300°F/ Gas 2. Cut the steak into small dice. Heat the oil in a large, flameproof casserole. Add the onion, garlic and green chilli and cook gently for 5 minutes until soft. Transfer the mixture to a plate.

3 Increase the heat to high, add the meat to the casserole and brown on all sides, then stir in the paprika, ground cumin and ground coriander.

4 Add the tomatoes, beef stock, dried chilli and hot pepper sauce. Drain the beans and add them to the casserole, with enough water to cover. Bring to simmering point, cover and cook in the oven for about 2 hours. Stir occasionally and add extra water, if necessary, to prevent the casserole from drying.

5 Season the casserole with salt and add the chopped red pepper. Replace the lid, return the casserole to the oven and cook for about 30 minutes more, or until the meat and beans are tender. Sprinkle over the fresh coriander and serve with boiled rice.

VARIATION
Use minced (ground) beef in place of the braising steak.

COOK'S TIP
Red kidney beans are traditionally used in chilli con carne, but in this recipe black beans are used instead. They are the same shape and size as red kidney beans but have a shiny black skin.

MEXICAN SPICY BEEF TORTILLA

THIS DISH IS NOT UNLIKE A LASAGNE, EXCEPT THAT THE SPICY MEAT IS MIXED WITH RICE AND IS LAYERED BETWEEN MEXICAN TORTILLAS, WITH A HOT SALSA SAUCE FOR AN EXTRA KICK.

SERVES FOUR

INGREDIENTS
1 onion, chopped
2 garlic cloves, crushed
1 fresh red chilli, seeded and
  thinly sliced
350g/12oz rump (round) steak, cut
  into small cubes
15ml/1 tbsp oil
225g/8oz/2 cups cooked long
  grain rice
beef stock, to moisten
3 large wheat tortillas
For the salsa picante
2 x 400g/14oz cans chopped
  tomatoes
2 garlic cloves, halved
1 onion, quartered
1–2 fresh red chillies, seeded and
  roughly chopped
5ml/1 tsp ground cumin
2.5–5ml/½–1 tsp cayenne pepper
5ml/1 tsp fresh oregano or 2.5ml/
  ½ tsp dried oregano
tomato juice or water, if required
For the cheese sauce
50g/2oz/4 tbsp butter
50g/2oz/½ cup plain (all-purpose)
  flour
600ml/1 pint/2½ cups milk
115g/4oz/1 cup grated Cheddar
  cheese
salt and ground black pepper

1 Preheat the oven to 180°C/350°F/ Gas 4. Make the salsa picante. Place the tomatoes, garlic, onion and chillies in a blender or food processor and process until smooth. Pour into a small pan, add the spices and oregano and season with salt.

2 Gradually bring the mixture to the boil, stirring occasionally. Boil for 1– 2 minutes, then lower the heat, cover with a lid and simmer gently for about 15 minutes. The sauce should be thick, but of a pouring consistency. If it is too thick, dilute it with a little fresh tomato juice or water.

3 Make the cheese sauce. Melt the butter in a pan and stir in the flour. Cook for 1 minute. Add the milk, stirring all the time until the sauce boils and thickens. Stir in all but 30ml/2 tbsp of cheese and season to taste. Cover the pan with a lid and set aside.

4 Mix the onion, garlic and chilli in a bowl. Add the steak cubes and mix well.

5 Heat the oil in a frying pan and stir-fry the meat mixture for about 10 minutes, until the meat cubes have browned and the onion is soft. Stir in the rice and enough beef stock to moisten. Season to taste with salt and freshly ground black pepper.

6 Pour about a quarter of the cheese sauce into the bottom of a round ovenproof dish. Add a tortilla and then spread over half the salsa followed by half the meat mixture.

7 Repeat these layers, then add half the remaining cheese sauce and the final tortilla. Pour over the remaining cheese sauce and sprinkle the reserved grated cheese on top. Bake in the preheated oven for about 15–20 minutes, or until golden on top.

SPICY MEATBALLS WITH TOMATO SAUCE

WHEREVER YOU GO IN LATIN AMERICA, YOU'LL FIND A DIFFERENT INTERPRETATION OF THIS HEARTY FAMILY DISH. SPANISH IN ORIGIN, THE MEATBALLS ARE OFTEN MADE WITH PORK OR VEAL, OR A MIXTURE OF MEATS, AND KNOWN AS ALBONDIGAS.

SERVES FOUR

INGREDIENTS
500g/1¼lb minced (ground) beef
3 garlic cloves, crushed
1 small onion, finely chopped
50g/2oz/1 cup fresh breadcrumbs
2.5ml/½ tsp ground cumin
1 egg, beaten
50g/2oz/½ cup plain
  (all-purpose) flour
60ml/4 tbsp olive oil
salt
cooked white rice, to serve
For the sauce
30ml/2 tbsp olive oil
1 small onion, thinly sliced
2 red (bell) peppers, seeded
  and diced
2 fresh red chillies, seeded
  and chopped
2 garlic cloves, crushed
150ml/¼ pint/⅔ cup canned
  chopped tomatoes
400ml/14fl oz/1⅔ cups light
  beef stock
ground black pepper

COOK'S TIP
An electric frying pan is ideal for cooking the meatballs, as its large surface area will allow you to fry them in one or two batches, and there is plenty of room for reheating them in the sauce.

1 Place all the meatball ingredients, except the flour and oil, in a large bowl. Using your hands, mix until thoroughly combined. Season with salt and shape the mixture into even-size balls. Wet your hands to prevent the mixture from sticking. Dust lightly with flour.

2 Heat the oil in a large frying pan and cook the meatballs, in batches, for 6–8 minutes or until golden. When all the meatballs have been browned, wipe the pan clean with kitchen paper.

3 Pour the olive oil into the pan and cook the onion and peppers over a low heat for 10 minutes, until soft. Add the chillies and garlic, and cook for a further 2 minutes. Pour in the tomatoes and stock, and bring to the boil. Lower the heat, cover the pan and simmer for 15 minutes. Season to taste.

4 Add the meatballs to the pan and spoon the sauce over them. Bring back to the boil, then cover and simmer for 10 minutes. Serve with rice.

SCRAMBLED EGGS WITH CHORIZO

THIS POPULAR MEXICAN DISH IS OFTEN EATEN FOR BREAKFAST. DRIED, SPANISH-STYLE CHORIZO GIVES THE EGGS A RICH GOLDEN COLOUR AND DELICIOUS SMOKY FLAVOUR. BUY THE SAUSAGE IN ONE PIECE AND SLICE IT JUST BEFORE COOKING.

SERVES FOUR

INGREDIENTS
15ml/1 tbsp olive oil
150g/5oz dried chorizo, cut into
  1cm/½in slices
2.5ml/½ tsp paprika
8 eggs, lightly beaten
salt
country bread and green salad,
  to serve

VARIATION
For extra fire and spice, add a dash of a hot pepper sauce, such as Tabasco, to the beaten egg mixture.

1 Heat the oil in a large frying pan over a medium heat and pan-fry the chorizo slices for 1–2 minutes, until browned and crisp.

COOK'S TIP
The chorizo will brown very quickly, so do not leave it to cook unattended, or it may burn.

2 Add the paprika, stir for 30 seconds, then pour in the beaten eggs. Season lightly with salt. As the eggs start to set, break them up with a fork.

3 Remove the pan from the heat when the mixture is still quite moist; it will continue cooking off the heat. Serve with the bread and a green salad.

SPICED ROAST LEG OF LAMB

PEPPERS AND BEANS ARE DELICIOUS COOKED WITH THIS SPICED LAMB — THE BEANS SOAK UP THE MEAT JUICES AND COMBINE WITH SWEET RED PEPPERS TO MAKE A SUCCULENT ONE-POT MEAL.

SERVES SIX

INGREDIENTS

  1 leg of lamb, about 1.8kg/4lb
  4 garlic cloves, crushed
  5ml/1 tsp ground cumin
  10ml/2 tsp ground annatto
   (achiote) seeds
  10ml/2 tbsp sweet paprika
  5ml/1 tsp dried oregano
  45ml/3 tbsp olive oil
  3 red (bell) peppers, cored, seeded
   and thickly sliced
  2 x 400g/14oz can black-eyed beans
   (peas), drained
  105ml/7 tbsp dry white wine
  salt and ground black pepper
  cooked white rice or polenta, to serve

COOK'S TIP
Look for ground annatto in South American or Caribbean markets, or replace with saffron or turmeric.

1 Weigh the lamb and calculate the cooking time. For medium-cooked lamb, allow 20 minutes per 450g/1lb, plus 20 minutes. Allow either 5 minutes more or less per 450/1lb for rare and well-done meat.

2 Mix the garlic, cumin, annatto, paprika and oregano in a bowl. Stir in half the olive oil. Using a spoon, rub the paste all over the lamb. Cover and marinate in a cool place for 2–3 hours.

3 Preheat the oven to 180ºC/350ºF/ Gas 4. Place the lamb in a roasting pan with the peppers and beans. Pour in the wine and drizzle with the remaining oil. Season, then roast for the calculated time. Check occasionally, adding water if the vegetables begin to dry out.

4 When the lamb is cooked, remove from the oven and cover the meat loosely with foil. Leave to rest for 15 minutes, then serve with rice or polenta.

RABBIT IN COCONUT MILK

THIS UNUSUAL DISH COMES FROM COLOMBIA. THE RABBIT IS STEWED IN A LIGHTLY SPICED TOMATO SAUCE, AND WHEN IT IS ALMOST READY, COCONUT MILK IS STIRRED IN TO ENRICH THE SAUCE.

SERVES FOUR

INGREDIENTS

1 rabbit, cut into 8 pieces (ask your
 butcher to do this for you)
3 garlic cloves, crushed
1.5ml/¼ tsp paprika
1.5ml/¼ tsp ground cumin
45ml/3 tbsp olive oil
1 large onion, thinly sliced
1 bay leaf
400g/14oz can plum tomatoes,
 drained and roughly chopped
150ml/¼ pint/⅔ cup chicken stock
250ml/8fl oz/1 cup coconut milk
salt and ground black pepper
white rice or boiled potatoes, to serve

3 Add the rabbit to the oil remaining in the pan, season and cook until golden. Do this over a very low heat to avoid burning the spices.

4 Return the onion slices to the pan and add the bay leaf. Stir in the tomatoes and stock and bring to the boil. Lower the heat, cover and simmer for 45 minutes.

VARIATION
This dish is often made with chicken rather than rabbit. The ingredients remain the same, but the cooking time should be reduced by 15 minutes.

5 Stir in the coconut milk. Continue to simmer, uncovered, for a further 15 minutes, until the rabbit is tender and the sauce has thickened. Serve immediately with white rice or boiled potatoes.

1 Wash the rabbit under cold water, then pat the pieces dry with kitchen paper. Combine the garlic, paprika and cumin in a bowl and rub the mixture all over the rabbit. Cover with clear film (plastic wrap) and leave to marinate for 1 hour, or overnight in the refrigerator.

2 Heat the oil in a pan, add the onion slices and cook for 5 minutes, until tender. Remove the onion with a slotted spoon and set aside.

PORK ROASTED WITH HERBS, SPICES AND RUM

IN THE CARIBBEAN, THIS SPICY ROAST PORK IS A FAVOURITE DISH THAT IS USUALLY COOKED ON A BARBECUE AND SERVED ON SPECIAL OCCASIONS AS PART OF A BUFFET.

SERVES EIGHT

INGREDIENTS
    2 garlic cloves, crushed
    45ml/3 tbsp soy sauce
    15ml/1 tbsp malt vinegar
    15ml/1 tbsp finely chopped celery
    30ml/2 tbsp chopped spring
      onion (scallion)
    7.5ml/1½ tsp dried thyme
    5ml/1 tsp dried sage
    2.5ml/½ tsp ground mixed spice
      (pumpkin pie spice)
    10ml/2 tsp curry powder
    120ml/4fl oz/½ cup rum
    15ml/1 tbsp demerara (raw) sugar
    1.6kg/3½lb boned loin of pork
    salt and ground black pepper
    spring onion (scallion) curls,
      to garnish
    creamed sweet potato, to serve
For the sauce
    25g/1oz/2 tbsp butter or
      margarine, diced
    15ml/1 tbsp tomato purée (paste)
    300ml/½ pint/1¼ cups chicken or
      pork stock
    15ml/1 tbsp chopped fresh parsley
    15ml/1 tbsp demerara (raw) sugar
    hot pepper sauce, to taste

1 In a bowl, mix the garlic, soy sauce, vinegar, celery, spring onion, thyme, sage, spice, curry powder, rum, and sugar. Add a little salt and pepper.

2 Open out the pork and slash the meat, without cutting through it completely. Place it in a shallow dish. Spread most of the spice mixture all over the pork, pressing it well into the slashes. Rub the outside of the joint with the remaining mixture, cover the dish with clear film (plastic wrap) and chill in the refrigerator overnight.

COOK'S TIP

In the Caribbean, pork is baked until it is very well done, so reduce the cooking time if you prefer meat slightly more moist. To get the full flavour from the marinade, start preparation the day before.

3 Preheat the oven to 190ºC/375ºF/ Gas 5. Roll the meat up, then tie it tightly in several places with strong cotton string to hold the meat together.

4 Spread a large piece of foil across a roasting pan and place the marinated pork loin in the centre. Baste the pork with a few spoonfuls of the marinade and wrap the foil around the meat.

5 Roast the pork in the oven for 1¾ hours, then slide the foil out from under the meat and discard it. Baste the pork with any remaining marinade and cook for a further 1 hour. Check occasionally that the meat is not drying out and baste with the pan juices.

6 Meanwhile, make the sauce. Transfer the pork to a warmed serving dish, cover with foil and leave to stand in a warm place for 15 minutes. Pour the pan juices into a pan. Add the butter or margarine, tomato purée, stock, parsley and sugar, with hot pepper sauce and salt to taste. Simmer until reduced.

7 Serve the pork sliced, with the creamed sweet potato. Garnish with the spring onion curls and serve the sauce separately.

PORK <u>WITH</u> PINEAPPLE

THIS UNUSUAL DISH FROM MEXICO COMBINES THE SWEET, JUICY TASTE OF FRESH PINEAPPLE WITH FIERY HOT CHILLIES, AND THE REFRESHING TANG OF COOL MINT.

SERVES SIX

INGREDIENTS

    30ml/2 tbsp corn oil
    900g/2lb boneless pork shoulder or
      loin, cut into 5cm/2in cubes
    1 onion, finely chopped
    1 large red (bell) pepper, seeded and
      finely chopped
    1 or more jalapeño chillies, seeded
      and finely chopped
    450g/1lb fresh pineapple chunks
    8 fresh mint leaves, chopped
    250ml/8fl oz/1 cup chicken stock
    salt and ground black pepper
    fresh mint sprigs, to garnish
    boiled rice, to serve

3 Add the mint, then cover the casserole with a tight-fitting lid and simmer gently for about 2 hours, or until the pork is tender.

4 Season to taste, garnish the casserole with fresh sprigs of mint and serve with plain boiled rice. Serve immediately, while still hot.

COOK'S TIP
If fresh pineapple is not available, use pineapple chunks from a can. Make sure it is canned in its own juice, however, and not in syrup or other fruit juice.

1 Heat the oil in a large frying pan and sauté the pork in batches until the cubes are lightly coloured. Transfer the pork to a flameproof casserole, leaving the oil behind in the pan.

2 Add the chopped onion, red pepper and the chillies to the oil remaining in the pan. Sauté until the onion is tender, then add to the casserole with the pineapple. Stir to mix.

CARBONADA CRIOLLA

MEAT AND FRUIT ARE OFTEN COMBINED IN ARGENTINIAN COOKING, AND THIS COLOURFUL STEW IS A PRIME EXAMPLE. THE TENDER BEEF COOKED IN RED WINE BALANCES THE SWEETNESS OF THE PEACHES, POTATOES AND PUMPKIN. MAKE SURE THE PUMPKIN FITS IN YOUR OVEN.

SERVES EIGHT

INGREDIENTS

1 large pumpkin, about 5kg/11lb
60ml/4 tbsp olive oil
1kg/2¼lb braising steak, cut into
   2.5cm/1in cubes
1 large onion, finely chopped
3 fresh red chillies, seeded
   and chopped
2 garlic cloves, crushed
1 large tomato, roughly chopped
2 fresh bay leaves
600ml/1 pint/2½ cups beef stock
350ml/12fl oz/1½ cups red wine
500g/1¼lb potatoes, peeled and cut
   into 2cm/¾in cubes
500g/1¼lb sweet potatoes, peeled
   and cut into 2cm/¾in cubes
1 corn cob, cut widthways into
   6 slices
3 peaches, peeled, stoned (pitted)
   and cut into thick wedges
salt and ground black pepper

1 Wash the outside of the pumpkin. Using a sharp knife, carefully cut a slice off the top 6cm/2½in from the stem, to make a lid. Using a spoon, scoop out the seeds and stringy fibres and discard. Scoop out some of the flesh, leaving a shell about 2cm/¾in thick inside of the pumpkin. Cut the flesh you have removed into 1cm/½in pieces.

COOK'S TIP
Calabaza is a large West Indian pumpkin with a greenish orange skin that is often used for *carbonada criolla*. Look for it in Caribbean markets.

2 Brush the inside of the pumpkin and the flesh side of the lid with a little olive oil. Season with salt and ground black pepper. Place both pumpkin and lid on a baking sheet, flesh-side up. Set aside.

3 Preheat the oven to 200°C/400°F/ Gas 6. Heat half the remaining oil in a large heavy pan over a high heat. Add the beef, season and sauté for 8–10 minutes, until golden brown, then remove with a slotted spoon – you may need to do this in batches. Avoid adding too much beef to the pan or it will steam rather than brown.

4 Lower the heat and add the remaining oil to the pan. Stir in the onion and chillies, and sauté for 5 minutes. Scrape the base of the pan with a wooden spoon, to loosen any sediment. Add the garlic and tomato and cook for 2 minutes more.

5 Return the meat to the pan and add the bay leaves, stock and red wine. Bring to the boil, then lower the heat to a gentle simmer. Cook for 1 hour or until the meat is tender.

6 Place the baking sheet containing the pumpkin and its lid in the oven and bake for 30 minutes.

7 Add the potatoes, sweet potatoes, pieces of pumpkin and corn to the stew. Pour in more liquid if needed and bring to the boil. Reduce the heat to a simmer, cover and cook for 15 minutes.

8 Finally add the peach wedges and season with salt and black pepper to taste. Spoon the stew into the partially cooked pumpkin, cover with the pumpkin lid and bake for 15 minutes or until the pumpkin is tender.

9 Carefully lift the filled pumpkin on to a large, strong platter and take it to the table. Ladle the stew on to plates, then cut the empty pumpkin into six to eight wedges, depending on the number of people to be served.

POULTRY

Chicken is the meat most frequently eaten in Latin America.
Chicken pie is perfect for a Sunday lunch, but for a delicious weekday meal
try fuss-free chicken with okra. Colombian chicken hot-pot and Peruvian
chicken, pork and potatoes in peanut sauce, are both national dishes.
Turkey and duck are also popular throughout the region.

CHICKEN PIE

THIS IS A GREAT FAMILY MEAL, PERFECT FOR A SUNDAY LUNCH. THE FILLING, WHICH INCLUDES CAPERS, OLIVES AND RAISINS, PROVIDES A FLAVOURSOME CONTRAST TO THE CRISP CORN TOPPING.

SERVES SIX

INGREDIENTS
  1 chicken, about 1.6kg/3½lb
  6 peppercorns
  1 bay leaf
  3 fresh parsley sprigs
  30ml/2 tbsp olive oil
  1 large onion, finely chopped
  2 hard-boiled eggs, chopped
  2 tomatoes, roughly chopped
  50g/2oz/½ cup pitted green olives,
    roughly chopped
  15ml/1 tbsp drained bottled capers
  65g/2½oz/scant ½ cup raisins
  salt and ground black pepper
For the topping
  500g/1¼lb/3⅓ cups drained canned
    or thawed frozen corn kernels
  90g/3½oz butter
  10ml/2 tsp caster (superfine) sugar
  3 eggs, lightly beaten
  salt

1 Put the chicken in a large, heavy pan and add enough water to cover. Add the peppercorns, bay leaf and parsley and bring to the boil over a high heat. Lower the heat, cover and simmer gently for 1 hour or until cooked through.

2 Allow the chicken to cool in the cooking liquid. When cold enough to handle, lift the chicken out of the pan and, using two forks, shred the flesh roughly. Discard the skin and bones.

3 Make the topping. Tip the corn kernels into a blender or food processor and purée until smooth. Melt the butter in a pan over a low heat. Stir in the puréed corn and sugar. Season generously with salt and cook, stirring, for 10 minutes, until the mixture thickens and comes away from the sides of the pan.

4 Remove from the heat and leave to cool for 10 minutes, then slowly stir in the beaten eggs, a little at a time. Set the topping mixture aside.

5 Preheat the oven to 180°C/350°F/ Gas 4. Heat the oil in a large frying pan and stir in the chopped onion. Cook gently for 5 minutes, until soft and translucent, and season with salt and black pepper to taste.

6 Stir in the chopped hard-boiled eggs, chopped tomatoes, olives, capers and raisins. Fold in the shredded chicken, making sure that it is well distributed throughout the mixture.

7 Spoon the pie filling into a 25 x 20cm/ 10 x 8in baking dish. Using a spoon, spread the corn topping evenly over the top of the chicken filling and bake for 45 minutes, until golden brown. Leave to stand for about 10 minutes before serving on warm plates.

VARIATION
Shortcrust pastry can be used instead of the corn topping.

CHICKEN WITH OKRA

SERVE THIS CLASSIC BRAZILIAN DISH FOR A FAMILY SUPPER. IT IS TOTALLY FUSS-FREE, TAKING VERY LITTLE TIME AND EFFORT TO PREPARE.

SERVES FOUR

INGREDIENTS

    15ml/1 tbsp olive oil
    4 chicken thighs
    1 large onion, finely chopped
    2 garlic cloves, finely crushed
    2 fresh red chillies, seeded and
      finely chopped
    120ml/4fl oz/½ cup water
    350g/12oz okra
    2 large tomatoes, finely chopped
    salt
    boiled white rice or polenta, to serve
    hot chilli oil (optional)

COOK'S TIP

As okra cooks, the pods release a sticky juice, which coats and flavours the chicken. If you don't like this sticky texture, however, cook the pods whole, simply trimming off the tops but not cutting into the pods themselves.

1 Heat the oil in a wide pan over a low heat. Season the chicken thighs with salt and add them to the pan, skin side down. Cook until golden brown, turn them over and add the chopped onion.

2 Sauté for 5 minutes, until the onion has softened; then add the garlic and chopped chillies. Cook for a further 2 minutes. Add half the water to the pan and bring to the boil. Lower the heat, cover and cook for 30 minutes.

3 Trim the okra and slice into thin rounds. Add to the pan with the tomatoes. Season with salt and pour in the remaining water. Cover and simmer gently for about 10–15 minutes, or until the chicken pieces are tender and fully cooked. The chicken is ready when the flesh can be pulled off the bone easily.

4 Serve immediately with boiled white rice or polenta, and offer some hot chilli oil on the side.

COLOMBIAN CHICKEN HOT-POT

COLOMBIANS ARE JUSTIFIABLY PROUD OF THIS NATIONAL DISH. TRADITIONALLY, THREE NATIVE VARIETIES OF POTATOES ARE USED, EACH WITH A DIFFERENT TEXTURE, TO CREATE A TASTY THICK BROTH. THE ADDITION OF CORIANDER AND CORN PROVIDES A COMPLEMENTARY SWEETNESS.

SERVES EIGHT

INGREDIENTS

1.6kg/3½lb chicken
3 spring onions (scallions)
2 bay leaves
6 fresh coriander (cilantro) sprigs
6 whole black peppercorns
675g/1½lb floury potatoes, peeled
  and cut into 1cm/½in chunks
675g/1½lb waxy potatoes, peeled
  and cut into 1cm/½in chunks
675g/1½lb baby new potatoes or
  salad potatoes
2 corn cobs, each cut into 4 pieces
salt
capers and sour cream, to serve
For the avocado salsa
1 hard-boiled egg
1 large ripe avocado
1 spring onion (scallion), finely
  chopped
15ml/1 tbsp chopped fresh
  coriander (cilantro)
1 fresh green chilli, seeded and
  finely chopped
salt

1 Put the chicken in a large pan or flameproof casserole and cover with water. Add the spring onions (scallions), bay leaves, coriander sprigs and peppercorns. Season, bring to the boil and skim the surface of the liquid.

2 Reduce the heat to a gentle simmer, cover and cook for 1 hour or until the chicken is tender and fully cooked. Remove from the heat and allow the chicken to cool in the cooking liquid.

3 Drain the chicken, reserving the cooking liquid to use as stock. Place the chicken on a board and cut it into 8 pieces. It should be so tender that the legs are easy to pull off.

4 Separate the thighs from the drumsticks. Use a knife to cut between the two breasts, then gently ease the meat off the bone. Cut the breasts in half, set the chicken pieces aside on a plate and discard the rest of the carcass.

5 Skim the fat from the top of the cooking liquid, then strain it into a clean pan. Bring to the boil. Add the floury and waxy potatoes and simmer for 15 minutes. Stir in the new potatoes or salad potatoes and corn and simmer for a further 20 minutes.

6 By this time, the floury potatoes will have broken up and they will have helped to thicken the liquid. The waxy potatoes should be soft and partly broken. The new or salad potatoes should be tender but still whole. Return the chicken pieces to the pan and reheat gently but thoroughly.

7 Meanwhile, make the fresh avocado salsa. Peel and roughly chop the hard-boiled egg. Using a fork, mash it in a small bowl.

8 Just before serving, cut the avocado in half lengthways and, using a teaspoon, scoop the flesh into a separate bowl. Mash well with a fork, then stir in the chopped hard-boiled egg until thoroughly combined. Add the spring onion, fresh coriander and chilli, mix well, then season to taste with salt.

9 Serve the chicken mixture in a heated casserole or earthenware dish, with bowls of hot tomato salsa, capers and sour cream on the side, if you like.

COOK'S TIP
The quality and flavour of the chicken stock in this dish will depend entirely on what kind of chicken you use. It is worth spending a bit more and buying the best bird you can find, preferably free range, corn-fed or organic. You will really taste the difference.

CHICKEN, PORK AND POTATOES IN PEANUT SAUCE

THIS TRADITIONAL PERUVIAN DISH, KNOWN AS CARAPULCRA, IS MADE WITH PAPASECA (DRIED POTATOES), WHICH BREAK UP WHEN COOKED TO THICKEN THE SAUCE. THE SAME EFFECT IS ACHIEVED HERE BY USING FLOURY POTATOES, THE KIND THAT DISINTEGRATE WHEN COOKED FOR A LONG TIME.

SERVES SIX

INGREDIENTS

75g/3oz/¾ cup unsalted peanuts
60ml/4 tbsp olive oil
3 chicken breast portions, halved
500g/1¼lb boneless pork loin, cut
   into 2cm/¾in pieces
1 large onion, chopped
30–45ml/2–3 tbsp water
3 garlic cloves, crushed
5ml/1 tsp paprika
5ml/1 tsp ground cumin
500g/1¼lb floury potatoes, peeled
   and thickly sliced
550ml/18fl oz/scant 2½ cups
   vegetable stock
salt and ground black pepper
cooked rice, to serve
To garnish
2 hard-boiled eggs, sliced
50g/2oz/½ cup pitted black olives
chopped fresh flat leaf parsley

1 Place the peanuts in a large dry frying pan over a low heat. Toast for about 2–3 minutes, until golden all over. Watch them closely, shaking the pan frequently, as they have a tendency to burn. Leave to cool, then process in a food processor until finely ground.

2 Heat half the olive oil in a heavy pan. Add the chicken pieces, season with salt and ground black pepper and cook for 10 minutes, until golden brown all over. Transfer the pieces of chicken to a plate, using a slotted spoon.

3 Heat the remaining oil in the pan. When it is very hot, add the pork. Season and sauté for 3–4 minutes, until golden brown. Transfer to the plate containing the chicken pieces.

4 Lower the heat and stir the onion into the oil in the pan. Cook for 5 minutes, adding the water if it begins to stick. Stir in the garlic, paprika and cumin and cook for 1 minute more.

5 Add the potatoes, stir and cover the pan. Cook for 3 minutes. Add the peanuts and stock. Bring to the boil, and simmer gently for 20–30 minutes.

6 Return the chicken and pork to the pan and bring to the boil. Lower the heat, replace the lid and simmer for 6–8 minutes, until the meat is fully cooked. Avoid overcooking the meat or it will become tough and stringy.

7 Garnish the stew with the egg slices, black olives and chopped parsley. Serve with the rice.

COOK'S TIP
If you cannot locate unsalted peanuts, buy a pack of salted ready-roasted peanuts, wash them under cold running water, then pat dry and grind.

PERUVIAN DUCK WITH RICE

Duck is very popular in Peru. In this recipe, the rice is cooked in the same liquid as the duck, so it absorbs the aromatic flavours of the herbs and spices.

SERVES SIX

INGREDIENTS
   2 fresh red chillies, seeded
   4 garlic cloves, roughly chopped
   5 fresh coriander (cilantro) stalks
   5ml/1 tsp ground cumin
   3 duck legs
   salt and ground black pepper
   1 large onion, finely chopped
   650ml/1 pint/2½ cups chicken stock
   250ml/8fl oz/1 cup red wine
   350g/12oz/1¾ cups long grain rice
   115g/4oz/1 cup frozen peas, thawed
   15ml/1 tbsp chopped fresh coriander,
      to garnish

VARIATION
If you find duck too fatty for your tastes, try making this dish with chicken legs or rabbit. It will be just as delicious.

1 Put the fresh chillies, garlic cloves, coriander stalks and ground cumin in a blender or food processor and process to a thick paste.

2 Cut the duck legs in half to separate the thigh from the drumstick. Place in a large heavy pan with a tight-fitting lid. Place over a low heat. Season the duck with salt and ground black pepper. Cook until golden brown on all sides, set the duck aside and pour away most of the fat, leaving about 30ml/2 tbsp.

3 Add the onion to the pan and cook gently for 5 minutes. Stir in the chilli and coriander paste and cook for a further 2 minutes. Return the duck to the pan, pour in the stock and wine and bring to the boil. Cover, reduce the heat and simmer for 45 minutes.

4 Stir the rice into the pan, replace the lid and cook for 18–20 minutes. Stir in the peas and remove from the heat. Leave to stand for 5 minutes and serve with a sprinkling of chopped coriander.

DRUNKEN DUCK

This is a lovely dish for a dinner party. The duck and sweet potatoes cook in the red wine and warm spices, creating a rich, almost chocolate-like sauce.

SERVES FOUR

INGREDIENTS
   1 duck, about 2.25kg/5lb
   1 large onion, thinly sliced
   2.5ml/½ tsp crushed dried chillies
   2 garlic cloves, crushed
   1.5ml/¼ tsp ground cloves
   1.5ml/¼ tsp ground allspice
   2.5ml/½ tsp ground cinnamon
   800g/1¾lb sweet potatoes, peeled
      and cut into thick wedges
   250ml/8fl oz/1 cup red wine
   250ml/8fl oz/1 cup chicken stock
   salt and ground black pepper
   polenta or cooked rice, to serve

1 Preheat the oven to 200°C/400°F/ Gas 6. Season the inside and outside of the duck. Place the duck in a large flameproof casserole over a low heat and cook, turning occasionally, until the skin has released some of its fat and turned a rich golden brown. Transfer the duck to a plate.

2 Pour away most of the duck fat from the pan, leaving about 30ml/2 tbsp. Return the casserole to the heat, add the onion and crushed chillies and stir well to coat in the fat, incorporating any sediment on the bottom of the pan.

3 Cook for 5 minutes until the onion is soft and translucent. Stir in the garlic and spices and cook for 1 minute more.

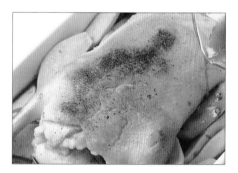

4 Return the duck to the casserole, arrange the sweet potatoes around it and pour in the wine and stock. Bring to the boil and cover. Move the dish to the oven and cook for 1¼–1½ hours.

5 Skim the fat from the top of the sauce and serve with soft polenta or plain rice.

VEGETARIAN DISHES AND SALADS

Although vegetarianism is not widespread in Latin America, root vegetables, corn and what might be considered exotic fruit and vegetables, such as heart of palm and okra are used extensively. The salads in this chapter can either be enjoyed as a light lunch, as an appetizer or as side dishes.

CORN SOUFFLÉ

LATIN AMERICAN SOUFFLÉS ARE QUITE DIFFERENT FROM THEIR FRENCH COUNTERPARTS. FOR EXAMPLE, THIS ONE WILL RISE ONLY SLIGHTLY, YET THE TEXTURE WILL STILL BE LIGHT AND AIRY.

SERVES SIX

INGREDIENTS
75g/3oz/6 tbsp butter
300g/11oz sweet potato, peeled
  and cubed
300g/11oz pumpkin, peeled
  and cubed
300g/11oz/scant 2 cups frozen corn
  kernels, thawed
3 spring onions (scallions),
  roughly chopped
150g/5oz Cheddar cheese, grated
5 eggs
salt and ground black pepper

1 Preheat the oven to 180°C/350°F/ Gas 4. Using 15g/½oz/1 tbsp of the butter, grease a 28 x 18cm/11 x 7in baking dish. Cook the sweet potato and pumpkin in a pan of lightly salted boiling water for 10 minutes, until tender. Drain and set aside.

2 Put 250g/9oz/1½ cups of corn kernals into a food processor. Add the chopped spring onions and process until smooth. Melt the remaining butter in a pan and stir in the corn and onion mixture. Cook, stirring, over a low heat, for about 1–2 minutes.

3 Add the cheese, stirring until it has melted. Season generously with salt and pepper. Remove from the heat.

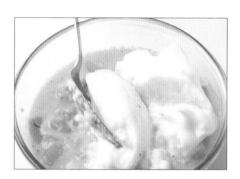

4 Separate three of the eggs and add the remaining whole eggs to the bowl containing the yolks. Mix lightly, then stir the yolk mixture into the pan. Add the sweet potato, pumpkin and remaining corn. Whisk the egg whites until stiff, then fold them into the soufflé mixture.

5 Transfer the mixture to the prepared dish and place the dish in a roasting pan. Pour in hot water to come halfway up the side of the dish and bake for 35–40 minutes, until golden. If the soufflé still wobbles when shaken gently, cook for a further 5–10 minutes. Leave to cool, then serve.

COOK'S TIP
For the best results, whisk the egg whites with a pinch of salt in a clean glass or metal bowl. When they are very stiff and no longer slide around the bowl when it is moved, they are ready for use.

LAYERED POTATO BAKE <u>WITH</u> CHEESE

INSPIRED BY THE PERUVIAN SIDE DISH, OCOPA AREQUIPENA, THIS FAMILY-SIZED POTATO CAKE IN A SPICY CHEESE AND WALNUT SAUCE IS SUBSTANTIAL ENOUGH FOR A MAIN COURSE.

4 Add the potatoes to a pan of salted water and cover. Bring to the boil, then simmer for 10 minutes. Drain and refresh under cold water. Drain again and cut into 1cm/½in slices. Shell the eggs and cut them into slices.

5 Preheat the oven to 180°C/350°F/ Gas 4. Grease a 28 x 18cm/11 x 7in baking dish with butter. Arrange a layer of potatoes in the dish and generously spread with the prepared paste. Top with egg slices and a sprinkling of olives and pimiento strips. Continue layering until all the ingredients have been used, finishing with olives and pimientos.

6 Bake for 30 minutes, until the potatoes are very tender. Leave to cool for 5 minutes before serving.

SERVES SIX

INGREDIENTS
  105ml/7 tbsp olive oil
  1 large onion, chopped
  2 garlic cloves, crushed
  5ml/1 tsp crushed dried chillies
  130g/4½oz/generous 1 cup
    walnut halves
  130g/4½oz/generous ½ cup fresh
    cheese, such as ricotta
  105ml/7 tbsp warm water
  3 eggs
  450g/1lb large potatoes, peeled
  butter, for greasing
  65g/2½oz/scant ¾ cup pitted
    black olives
  4 pimientos, cut into strips
  salt

1 Heat 30ml/2 tbsp of the oil in a small pan over a low heat. Add the chopped onion and sauté gently for 5 minutes, until softened. Stir in the garlic and crushed dried chillies and cook for a further 2 minutes.

2 Put the walnuts in a blender or food processor. Blend until smooth, then add the cooked onion mixture, with the cheese and remaining olive oil. Season generously with salt and pour in the warm water. Blend to make a smooth paste. Set aside.

3 Put the eggs in a small pan of cold water. Bring to the boil, then lower the heat to a simmer. Cook for 10 minutes then cool in a bowl of cold water.

HEART OF PALM PIE

THE DELICATE CREAMY FILLING IN THIS PIE CONTRASTS BEAUTIFULLY WITH THE CRUMBLY PASTRY. THIS RECIPE CAN ALSO BE USED TO MAKE SMALL BRAZILIAN EMPADINHAS — BABY SAVOURY PIES — NOT TO BE CONFUSED WITH EMPANADAS, THE LITTLE TURNOVERS.

SERVES EIGHT

INGREDIENTS
  500g/1¼lb/5 cups plain
    (all-purpose) flour
  5ml/1 tsp salt
  175g/6oz/¾ cup butter
  75g/3oz/6 tbsp lard or white
    cooking fat
  1 egg yolk
  45ml/3 tbsp cold water
For the filling
  25g/1oz/2 tbsp butter
  1 large onion, finely chopped
  4 garlic cloves, crushed
  15ml/1 tbsp plain (all-purpose) flour
  200ml/7fl oz/scant 1 cup full-fat
    (whole) milk
  2 hard-boiled eggs, roughly chopped
  1 large tomato, peeled, seeded
    and cubed
  1 fresh red chilli, seeded and
    finely chopped
  2 x 400g/14oz cans heart of palm,
    drained and cut into 2cm/¾in
    slices
  15ml/1 tbsp chopped fresh flat
    leaf parsley
  salt and ground black pepper
To glaze
  1 egg yolk
  15ml/1 tbsp water

1 Place the flour, salt, butter and lard or cooking fat in a food processor and process until the mixture resembles fine breadcrumbs. With the motor still running, add the egg yolk and the cold water. As soon as the mixture comes together, transfer to a floured surface. Knead it lightly until smooth. Divide the pastry into two rounds, one slightly larger than the other, wrap both in cling film (plastic wrap) and place in the refrigerator while you make the filling.

2 Melt the butter in a frying pan over a low heat. Stir in the chopped onion and cook for 5 minutes until soft. Add the garlic and cook for a further 2 minutes.

3 Stir the flour into the pan and cook, stirring, for 1 minute. Remove from the heat and slowly pour in the milk, a little at a time, stirring to prevent any lumps from forming.

4 Return to the heat and cook, stirring constantly, for 2 minutes to make a thin white sauce. Remove from the heat and stir in the chopped hard-boiled eggs, cubed tomato, chilli, palm hearts and parsley. Season with salt and pepper.

5 Preheat the oven to 190°C/375°F/Gas 5. Place a large baking sheet on the central shelf so that it heats up.

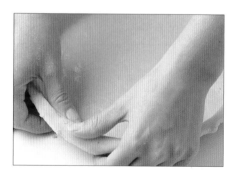

6 On a floured surface, roll out the larger piece of pastry and line the base and sides of a 23cm/9in round loose-based quiche pan. The pastry will be very crumbly, so it may tear in a few places. Should this happen, use your fingers to push the pastry together again. There should be no gaps.

7 Add the filling, then roll out the remaining pastry and use to top the pie. Do not worry about any small gaps in the pastry, as they add to the rustic character of the dish.

8 Make the glaze by mixing the egg yolk with the water. Using a pastry brush glaze the pastry, then place the quiche pan on the heated baking sheet and bake the pie for 45 minutes, until the pastry is golden.

9 Leave the pie to cool for 5 minutes on a wire rack before removing it from the pan and putting it on to a large plate. Serve warm or at room temperature.

COOK'S TIP
Cooking the pie on a heated baking sheet ensures that the pastry cooks thoroughly, avoiding a soggy base.

AVOCADO AND GRAPEFRUIT SALAD

THIS IS A LIGHT, REFRESHING LUNCH-TIME SALAD. THE BUTTERY TEXTURE OF THE AVOCADOS, COMBINES WITH THE TANGINESS OF THE GRAPEFRUIT TO MAKE THE PERFECT SUMMER DISH. SERVE IT AS A LIGHT MAIN COURSE OR AS AN ACCOMPANIMENT TO BARBECUED MEATS.

SERVES FOUR

INGREDIENTS
   90ml/6 tbsp olive oil
   30ml/2 tbsp white wine vinegar
   1 pink grapefruit
   2 large ripe avocados
   1 cos or romaine lettuce, separated
      into leaves
   salt and ground black pepper

1 Using a balloon whisk or a fork, whisk the olive oil and white wine vinegar together in a large bowl, season to taste with salt and ground black pepper and vigorously whisk again.

VARIATIONS
Try other fruit combinations. Mango and strawberries go well together, as do papaya and limes.

2 Slice the top and bottom off the grapefruit. Peel the fruit by running a small knife all around it, between peel and flesh. Make sure all the bitter pith is removed. Hold the grapefruit over the bowl containing the dressing and cut carefully between the membranes, so that all the segments fall into the bowl. Squeeze the remaining pulp over the bowl to extract all the juice.

3 Run a knife around the length of the avocados. Twist the sides in opposite directions to separate the halves. Use a large spoon to remove the stone (pit), then peel the halves. Slice the flesh and cover these with the dressing, to stop them from discolouring.

4 Tear the lettuce into pieces and add to the bowl. Toss to coat. Adjust the seasoning to taste and serve.

QUINOA SALAD WITH CITRUS DRESSING

QUINOA IS A TYPE OF GRAIN GROWN IN THE ANDES. A STAPLE FOOD OF THE REGION, IT HAS BEEN CULTIVATED SINCE THE TIME OF THE INCAS AND AZTECS. QUINOA IS PACKED WITH PROTEIN AND IS ALSO GLUTEN FREE, SO IT IS IDEAL FOR VEGETARIANS AND THOSE WHO ARE GLUTEN INTOLERANT.

SERVES SIX

INGREDIENTS
175g/6oz/1 cup quinoa
90ml/6 tbsp olive oil
juice of 2 limes
juice of 1 large orange
2 fresh green chillies, seeded and
  finely chopped
2 garlic cloves, crushed
½ cucumber, peeled
1 large tomato, seeded and cubed
4 spring onions (scallions), sliced
30ml/2 tbsp chopped fresh mint
15ml/1 tbsp chopped fresh flat
  leaf parsley
salt

COOK'S TIP
Quinoa can also be eaten plain as an accompaniment to meat or fish dishes.

1 Put the quinoa in a sieve (strainer), rinse thoroughly under cold water, then tip into a large pan. Pour in cold water to cover and bring to the boil. Lower the heat and simmer for 10–12 minutes, until tender. Drain and leave to cool.

2 Make a dressing by whisking the oil with the citrus juices. Stir in the chillies and garlic and season with salt.

3 Cut the cucumber in half lengthways and, using a teaspoon, scoop out and discard the seeds. Cut into 5mm/¼in slices and add to the cooled quinoa with the tomato, spring onions and herbs. Toss well to combine.

4 Pour the dressing over the salad and toss again until well mixed. Check the seasoning and serve.

OKRA AND TOMATO SALAD

FOR THIS SALAD THE OKRA IS COOKED AS LITTLE AS POSSIBLE, KEEPING IT CRUNCHY. SERVE AS A SIDE SALAD, OR STIR IN SOME BABY SPINACH FOR A MEMORABLE MAIN COURSE.

SERVES FOUR

INGREDIENTS
  60ml/4 tbsp olive oil
  15ml/1 tbsp red wine vinegar
  1 red onion, very thinly sliced
  3 tomatoes, peeled and seeded
  400g/14oz okra
  salt and ground black pepper

1 In a large bowl, whisk together the olive oil and red wine vinegar. Season with salt and ground black pepper. Toss the slices of red onion into the dressing and leave to marinate while you prepare and cook the okra.

2 Trim the tough stalks from the okra, but avoid cutting into the pods, otherwise you will release a sticky liquid. Cook the okra in a pan of lightly salted boiling water for 4–5 minutes, until just tender. Drain and dry on kitchen paper. Leave the small okra whole, but cut any larger ones diagonally in half.

3 Stir the cooked okra into the dressing, mix thoroughly and leave to marinate for about 20–25 minutes.

4 Cut the tomatoes into thin wedges and add them to the bowl. Gently toss them together with the okra. Season to taste with salt and ground black pepper and serve immediately.

TOMATO, HEART OF PALM AND ONION SALAD

THIS SIMPLE SALAD CAN BE ASSEMBLED IN MINUTES. IT IS AN EXCELLENT DISH FOR INTRODUCING ANYONE TO THE DELICATE FLAVOUR OF PALM HEARTS.

SERVES FOUR

INGREDIENTS
  4 beefsteak tomatoes
  1 small onion, thinly sliced
  400g/14oz can hearts of palm
For the dressing
  juice of 1 lime
  10ml/2 tsp Dijon mustard
  60ml/4 tbsp olive oil
  salt and ground black pepper

1 Cut the tomatoes into 1cm/½in slices and arrange on a large serving platter. Sprinkle the thin onion slices over the tomatoes and season to taste with salt and ground black pepper.

3 Make the dressing by whisking the lime juice, mustard and oil in a bowl. Season with salt and ground pepper. Drizzle over the salad and serve.

COOK'S TIP
If the tomatoes are not perfectly ripe, sprinkle the slices with a large pinch of caster (superfine) sugar, to help bring out their sweetness.

2 Drain the canned hearts of palm thoroughly, cut them into 1cm/½in slices and sprinkle the slices over the tomatoes and onions.

VARIATION
If you cannot get hearts of palm, this salad will be just as delicious using artichoke hearts instead.

PERUVIAN SALAD

THIS IS A SPECTACULAR-LOOKING SALAD THAT COULD BE SERVED AS A SIDE DISH OR A LIGHT LUNCH.
IN PERU, WHITE RICE WOULD BE USED, BUT BROWN RICE ADDS AN INTERESTING TEXTURE AND FLAVOUR.

SERVES FOUR

INGREDIENTS
225g/8oz/2 cups cooked long grain
  brown or white rice
15ml/1 tbsp chopped fresh parsley
1 red (bell) pepper
1 small onion, sliced into rings
olive oil, for sprinkling
115g/4oz green beans, halved
50g/2oz/½ cup baby corn
4 quail's eggs, hard-boiled and halved
25–50g/1–2oz Spanish ham, cut into
  thin slices (optional)
1 small avocado
lemon juice, for sprinkling
75g/3oz mixed salad leaves
15ml/1 tbsp capers
about 10 stuffed olives, halved
For the dressing
1 garlic clove, crushed
60ml/4 tbsp olive oil
45ml/3 tbsp sunflower oil
30ml/2 tbsp lemon juice
45ml/3 tbsp natural (plain) yogurt
2.5ml/½ tsp mustard
2.5ml/½ tsp granulated sugar
salt and ground black pepper

1 Make the dressing by placing all the ingredients in a bowl and whisking with a fork or whisk until smooth. Alternatively, place the ingredients in an empty jam jar, screw the lid on tightly and shake well.

2 Put the cooked rice into a large, glass salad bowl and spoon in half the dressing. Add the chopped parsley, stir well and set aside.

3 Cut the pepper in half, remove the seeds and pith, then place the halves, cut side down, in a small roasting pan. Add the onion rings. Sprinkle the onion with a little olive oil, place the pan under a hot grill (broiler) and cook for 5–6 minutes until the pepper blackens and blisters and the onion turns golden. You may need to stir the onion once or twice so that it cooks evenly.

4 Stir the onion in with the rice. Put the pepper in a plastic bag and knot the bag. When the steam has loosened the skin on the pepper halves and they are cool enough to handle, peel them and cut the flesh into thin strips.

5 Cook the green beans in boiling water for 2 minutes, then add the corn and cook for 1–2 minutes more, until tender. Drain both vegetables, refresh them under cold water, then drain again. Place in a large mixing bowl and add the red pepper strips, quail's eggs and ham, if using.

6 Peel the avocado, remove the stone (pit), and cut the flesh into slices or chunks. Sprinkle with the lemon juice. Put the salad leaves in a separate mixing bowl, add the avocado and mix lightly. Arrange the salad leaves and avocado on top of the rice.

7 Stir about 45ml/3 tbsp of the dressing into the green bean and pepper mixture. Pile this on top of the salad.

8 Sprinkle the capers and stuffed olives on top and serve the salad with the remaining dressing.

PUMPKIN SALAD

RED WINE VINEGAR BRINGS OUT THE SWEETNESS OF THE PUMPKIN. NO SALAD LEAVES ARE USED, JUST PLENTY OF FRESH PARSLEY. EATEN THROUGHOUT LATIN AMERICA, IT IS GREAT FOR A COLD BUFFET.

SERVES FOUR

INGREDIENTS
    1 large red onion, peeled and very
    thinly sliced
    200ml/7fl oz/scant 1 cup olive oil
    60ml/4 tbsp red wine vinegar
    675g/1½lb pumpkin, peeled and cut
    into 4cm/1½in pieces
    40g/1½oz/¾ cup fresh flat leaf
    parsley leaves, chopped
    salt and ground black pepper

VARIATIONS
Try replacing the pumpkin with sweet
potatoes. Wild rocket (arugula) or fresh
coriander (cilantro) can be used instead
of the parsley, if you prefer.

1 Mix the onion, olive oil and vinegar in
a large bowl. Stir well to combine.

2 Put the pumpkin in a large pan of
cold salted water. Bring to the boil, then
lower the heat and simmer gently for
15–20 minutes. Drain.

3 Immediately add the drained pumpkin
to the bowl containing the dressing and
toss lightly with your hands. Leave to
cool. Stir in the chopped parsley, cover
with clear film (plastic wrap) and chill.
Allow the salad to come back to room
temperature before serving.

SIDE DISHES AND SALSAS

Traditionally, Latin American meals consist of a meat, fish or poultry dish accompanied by rice, beans or potatoes and side dishes, such as stir-fried spring greens. Salsa, whether hot and spicy with chilli or cool and refreshing, is served as a relish or stirred into dishes.

PLAIN RICE

RICE IS A STAPLE FOOD IN MANY PARTS OF LATIN AMERICA — IT IS EATEN AT MOST MEALS WITH ANYTHING AND EVERYTHING, AND IS OFTEN ACCOMPANIED BY BLACK BEANS.

SERVES FOUR

INGREDIENTS
  200g/7oz/1 cup long grain rice
  30ml/2 tbsp vegetable oil
  2 garlic cloves, crushed
  450ml/¾ pint/scant 2 cups water
  salt

COOK'S TIP

If the rice is still tough after steaming, add a little water, cover and return to the heat for a few minutes. If, instead, the rice is still sticky, return to the heat and cook over a very low heat with the lid off, until the excess moisture has evaporated.

1 Rinse the rice in a large bowl of cold water, then drain thoroughly in a fine sieve (strainer). Pour the oil into a heavy pan that has a tight-fitting lid. Heat gently, then add the garlic and cook, stirring, for 1 minute. Add the rice and stir for 2 minutes, until the grains are lightly toasted.

2 Pour in the water and season with salt. Bring to the boil, cover and lower the heat again to a very gentle simmer. Cook for 18 minutes, without lifting the lid. Remove from the heat and leave the rice to rest, covered, for 5 minutes. Transfer to a serving bowl and fluff up with a fork before taking to the table.

BLACK BEANS

YOU'LL FIND BEANS ON MOST LATIN TABLES, WHATEVER THE DAY OF THE WEEK OR OCCASION. THE RECIPE WILL VARY SLIGHTLY, DEPENDING ON THE COUNTRY, THE AVAILABILITY OF ADDITIONAL INGREDIENTS AND PERSONAL CHOICE. CHILLIES AND OTHER SPICES ARE OFTEN INCLUDED.

SERVES SIX

INGREDIENTS
  450g/1lb/2½ cups black turtle
    beans, soaked overnight in water to
    cover
  115g/4oz smoked streaky (fatty)
    bacon, in one piece
  1 bay leaf
  30ml/2 tbsp vegetable oil
  2 garlic cloves, crushed
  salt

COOK'S TIP

Do not season the beans until they are cooked, or they will become tough. As the sauce thickens, the beans have a tendency to stick, so stir frequently after returning the refried beans to the pan.

1 Drain the beans and put them in a large heavy pan. Cover generously with cold water. Add the bacon and bay leaf and bring to the boil. Skim the surface of the liquid, then lower the heat to a simmer. Cook for at least 1 hour or until the beans are tender, topping up the water if necessary.

2 Heat the oil in a pan over a medium heat. Cook the garlic for 2 minutes. Add two ladles of cooked beans and fry for 2–3 minutes, breaking up the beans.

3 Tip the refried beans back into the pan and season. Simmer over a very low heat for 10 minutes, then serve.

CASSAVA WITH A CITRUS SALSA

THIS DISH CONSISTS OF DICED CASSAVA IN A CLASSIC SAUCE CALLED MOJO. WHEN THE COOKED CASSAVA IS COATED IN THE SHARP DRESSING, IT BECOMES IMBUED WITH THE DELICIOUS FLAVOURS OF FRESH ORANGE, LIME AND GARLIC.

SERVES FOUR

INGREDIENTS
  800g/1¾lb cassava, peeled and cut
    into chunks
  2 garlic cloves, crushed
  juice of 1 small orange
  juice of 1 lime
  45ml/3 tbsp olive oil
  15ml/1 tbsp chopped fresh flat
    leaf parsley
  salt

VARIATION
Mojo is also delicious with cooked pumpkin and sweet potatoes.

1 Cook the cassava in a large pan of salted boiling water for 20–25 minutes, until beginning to break up. Drain in a colander and then transfer to a large serving plate.

2 Mix the garlic, orange juice and lime juice in a bowl. Whisk in the oil, season with salt and stir in the parsley. Drizzle the dressing over the cooked cassava and serve.

STIR-FRIED SPRING GREENS

SPRING GREENS ARE VERY POPULAR IN BRAZIL. THEY ARE EATEN WITH MEAT AND ARE THE TRADITIONAL ACCOMPANIMENT TO FEIJOADA. GARLIC ENHANCES THEIR SLIGHTLY BITTER FLAVOUR, AND THEY TASTE EVEN BETTER WHEN COOKED WITH BACON AND CHILLIES.

SERVES SIX

INGREDIENTS
    450g/1lb spring greens (collards)
    15ml/1 tbsp vegetable oil
    150g/5oz smoked streaky (fatty)
      bacon, in one piece
    2 garlic cloves, crushed
    1.5ml/¼ tsp crushed dried chillies
    salt

VARIATIONS
• If you cannot find spring greens, use curly kale or Savoy cabbage instead. These may not be as vibrant in colour, but the taste will be very similar.
• Cubed pancetta can be used instead of the bacon.

1 Cut off the hard stalks from the spring greens. Lay the leaves flat on top of each other and roll into a tight cigar-shape. Slice very thinly, using a sharp knife.

2 Heat the oil in a large frying pan over a low heat. Cut the bacon into small cubes and sauté in the oil for 5 minutes, or until golden brown. Lift the cubes out of the pan with a slotted spoon and drain on kitchen paper.

3 Increase the heat, add the crushed garlic and dried chillies to the oil remaining in the pan, and stir-fry for about 30 seconds.

4 Add the shredded spring greens and toss over the heat until just tender. Season to taste with salt, stir in the cooked bacon cubes and serve immediately.

ARGENTINIAN BARBECUE SALSA

*THIS COMBINATION OF FINELY CHOPPED VEGETABLES AND TART DRESSING IS THE PERFECT
PARTNER FOR ALL TYPES OF GRILLED MEATS, SO IT IS NOT SURPRISING TO FIND BOWLS OF FRESH
SALSA CREOLLA ON THE TABLE WHENEVER A BARBECUE OR ASADO IS BEING PEPARED. SIMILAR
BARBECUE SALSAS CAN ALSO BE FOUND IN BRAZIL, URUGUAY AND PARAGUAY.*

SERVES SIX

INGREDIENTS
  2 fresh green chillies, seeded and
    very finely chopped
  1 garlic clove, crushed
  1 onion, very finely chopped
  1 large tomato, peeled, seeded and
    very finely chopped
  15ml/1 tbsp finely chopped fresh flat
    leaf parsley
  salt
  105ml/7 tbsp olive oil
  30ml/2 tbsp red wine vinegar

1 Combine the chopped chillies,
crushed garlic, onion and tomato in a
bowl. Stir in the chopped parsley and
season to taste with salt.

2 Pour in the oil and vinegar and stir
well. Allow the flavours to mingle for at
least 1 hour before serving with grilled
(broiled) or barbecued meats.

HOT CHILLI SALSA

*CONTRARY TO POPULAR BELIEF, LATIN FOOD IS NOT INTRINSICALLY SPICY. IT IS THE HOT CHILLI OILS
AND SALSAS, ADDED TO DISHES AT THE TABLE, THAT FAN THE FLAMES.*

MAKES ONE SMALL JAR

INGREDIENTS
  10 fresh red chillies, roughly
    chopped
  1 large tomato, peeled and quartered
  2 garlic cloves
  juice of 1 lime
  60ml/4 tbsp olive oil
  salt

COOK'S TIP
Treat this salsa with extreme caution.
Just the oil is enough to add serious heat
to a dish, especially if the salsa has had
a chance to age. A couple of drops of the
oil are enough for most people!

1 Place the chillies, tomato and garlic
in a food processor, then process the
mixture until smooth.

2 Scrape the mixture into a small frying
pan and place over a medium heat.
Season with salt and cook, stirring, for
10 minutes, until the sauce is thick.

3 Remove from the heat and stir in the
freshly squeezed lime juice. Transfer to
a sterilized airtight jar and top with a
thin film of olive oil before tightly
screwing on the lid. As long as the
sauce always has a film of oil on top, it
will keep for ages at room temperature
or in the refrigerator.

TAMARILLO SAUCE

*THIS UNUSUAL PERUVIAN SAUCE MAKES A DELICIOUS DIP FOR SERVING WITH AREPAS — THOSE
IRRESISTIBLE CORN MEAL GRIDDLE CAKES THAT ARE FREQUENTLY FILLED WITH SOFT WHITE CHEESE.
ALTERNATIVELY, ITS DELICIOUS, HOT AND SPICY FLAVOUR CONTRASTS BEAUTIFULLY WITH THE
NATURAL SWEETNESS OF FRESH GRILLED SEAFOOD.*

SERVES FOUR

INGREDIENTS
    450g/1lb fresh tamarillos
    2.5ml/½ tsp ground ginger
    1.5ml/¼ tsp ground cinnamon
    1 fresh red chilli, seeded
      and chopped
    1 small onion, finely chopped
    5ml/1 tsp light brown sugar
    105ml/7 tbsp water
    30ml/2 tbsp olive oil
    salt

COOK'S TIP
If tamarillos are heavier than they look,
they will be ripe and juicy.

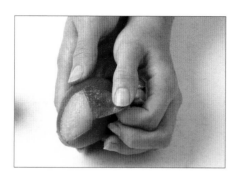

1 Place the whole fresh tamarillos in a
large pan of boiling water for about 30
seconds. Drain, refresh in cold water,
then carefully remove the peel with a
sharp knife and discard it. Roughly
chop the tamarillos.

2 Place the ginger and cinnamon in a
small heavy pan over a low heat. Stir
the mixture for 30 seconds, until the
spices release their aroma. Add the
chopped tamarillos, chilli, onion, sugar
and water.

3 Bring to the boil, lower the heat, cover
and simmer for 20 minutes. Remove the
lid and continue cooking until the sauce
thickens. Stir in the oil and season with
salt. Serve with grilled (broiled) seafood.

AVOCADO SALSA

THERE ARE MANY VERSIONS OF AVOCADO SALSA, INCLUDING THE CLASSIC MEXICAN GUACAMOLE. HERE THE INGREDIENTS ARE CHOPPED AND DICED, RATHER THAN MASHED, WHICH ADDS TEXTURE AND ALLOWS ALL THE DELICIOUS FLAVOURS TO REMAIN DISTINCT. PREPARE THIS SALSA AT THE LAST MINUTE TO AVOID THE AVOCADOS DISCOLOURING.

SERVES FOUR

INGREDIENTS
  1 large ripe avocado
  juice of 1 lime
  15ml/1 tbsp red wine vinegar
  1 tomato, peeled, seeded
    and chopped
  1 green (bell) pepper, seeded
    and diced
  1 red onion, finely chopped
  1 fresh red chilli, seeded and
    finely chopped
  45ml/3 tbsp olive oil
  salt

1 Prepare the avocado. Run a sharp knife around the whole length of the avocado, cutting right in until you touch the stone (pit). Twist the two sides of the split avocado in opposite directions to separate the two halves.

2 Use a large spoon to remove the large stone, then peel both halves of the avocado. Dice the flesh and put it in a bowl with the lime juice.

3 Stir the vinegar, tomato, pepper, onion and chilli into the avocado and lime juice mixture. Gradually add the olive oil, mixing well.

COOK'S TIP
If there is any delay before serving this salsa, add the avocado stone to the mixture. This will prevent any discoloration. Remember to remove the stone before serving though.

4 Season to taste with salt and serve with tortilla chips, or as an accompaniment to meat, fish or poultry.

DESSERTS

The abundant supply of sweet and juicy tropical fruit available in Latin America means that dessert usually consists of fresh fruit or fresh fruit dishes such as mango sorbet. Otherwise, desserts tend to be based on eggs and sugar and are usually of Spanish and Portuguese origin, where rich custard tarts and crème caramels have always been popular.

MANGO SORBET

THIS FOOLPROOF RECIPE IS INCREDIBLY EASY TO MAKE WITHOUT AN ICE-CREAM MAKER. A SMOOTH TEXTURE AND FRUITY, CONCENTRATED FLAVOUR IS GUARANTEED.

SERVES SIX

INGREDIENTS
200g/7oz/1 cup caster (superfine) sugar
150ml/¼ pint/⅔ cup water
3 large ripe mangoes
juice of 1 lime
1 egg white

COOK'S TIP
Home-made sorbets (sherbets) tend to set more solidly than bought versions, so always transfer them to the refrigerator to thaw slightly before serving.

VARIATION
The sorbet can be made with ripe papayas instead of mangoes. Add the grated rind of the lime as well as the juice.

1 Dissolve the sugar in the water in a small pan over a low heat. Allow to cool.

2 Cut off a thick lengthways slice from either side of each mango. Cut off any flesh, peel and chop it roughly. Put the mango flesh in a food processor or blender and process until smooth.

3 Scrape into a freezerproof bowl and stir in the syrup and lime juice. Freeze for 2–4 hours until almost solid.

4 Scoop into a food processor and blend until soft. Pour in the egg white and blend until combined. Return to the bowl, cover and freeze until firm.

COLOMBIAN PINEAPPLE CUSTARD

THESE PINEAPPLE CRÈME CARAMELS ARE THE PERFECT DINNER PARTY DESSERT. THEY ARE VERY EASY TO MAKE, ESPECIALLY IF YOU BUY PREPARED FRESH PINEAPPLE FROM THE SUPERMARKET.

MAKES SIX

INGREDIENTS
    350g/12oz peeled fresh
      pineapple, chopped
    150g/5oz/⅔ cup caster
      (superfine) sugar
    4 eggs, lightly beaten
For the caramel
    60ml/4 tbsp granulated sugar
    juice of 1 lime

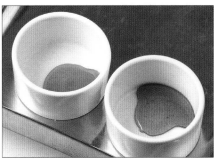

1 Put the pineapple in a blender or food processor and process until smooth. Scrape the purée into a pan and add the sugar. Cook for 5 minutes or until reduced by one-third. The mixture should be thick but not jam-like, so add a little water if it is too thick. Transfer to a bowl and leave to cool.

COOK'S TIP
Avoid over-whisking the eggs. Gently stir them into the pineapple mixture without incorporating air.

2 Meanwhile make the caramel. Place the granulated sugar in a heavy pan over a medium heat. As the sugar starts to caramelize around the edges, shake the pan to mix the sugar, but do not stir. Remove the pan from the heat as soon as all the sugar has dissolved and the caramel has become golden brown. Immediately stir in the lime juice taking care not to burn yourself. The hot caramel will spit when the lime juice is added, but this will stop. Divide the caramel among six ramekins and turn them so that they are coated evenly.

3 Preheat the oven to 180°C/350°F/ Gas 4. Stir the eggs into the cool pineapple mixture. Divide the mixture equally among the ramekins. Place the moulds in a roasting pan and pour in warm water to come halfway up their sides. Cover with foil and bake for 45 minutes, until set. Allow to cool.

4 Just before serving, unmould the custards directly on to dessert plates. Loosen the edges with a knife, invert a dessert plate on top of each mould and turn both over.

COCONUT AND PUMPKIN COMPOTE

LATIN AMERICANS LOVE WHOLE PRESERVED FRUITS IN SYRUP. ALSO POPULAR ARE COMPOTES LIKE THIS ONE, TRADITIONALLY SERVED WITH FRESH CHEESE.

SERVES SIX

INGREDIENTS
    800g/1¾lb pumpkin, peeled
      and seeded
    450g/1lb/2¼ cups caster
      (superfine) sugar
    4 cloves
    350ml/12fl oz/1½ cups water
    115g/4oz/1⅓ cups desiccated (dry
      unsweetened shredded) coconut
    ricotta cheese, to serve

VARIATION
This preserve is more traditionally made without coconut. For pure pumpkin compote, leave out the coconut and double the quantity of pumpkin.

1 Cut the pumpkin into even-size pieces and place in a heavy pan. Add the sugar, cloves and water. Heat gently, without bringing to the boil, until the sugar has dissolved.

2 Increase the heat to medium. Simmer the mixture for 30–35 minutes, until the pumpkin is soft. Using a fork mash the cooked pumpkin until it is reduced to a rough purée.

3 Stir in the coconut and simmer for a further 15 minutes. The mixture should be thick but still liquid, so add more water if necessary. Leave to cool, then transfer to an airtight container and store in the refrigerator for up to 2 weeks.

4 Spoon the compote into a serving bowl and allow it to come to room temperature before serving with a fresh white cheese, such as ricotta.

DULCE DE LECHE

SPANISH IN ORIGIN, THIS TOFFEE-LIKE DESSERT IS A CHILDREN'S FAVOURITE THROUGHOUT LATIN AMERICA. LITERALLY TRANSLATED AS "CARAMELIZED MILK", IT IS TRADITIONALLY MADE WITH MILK AND SUGAR, BUT THIS VERSION IS MUCH QUICKER AND JUST AS DELICIOUS.

SERVES SIX

INGREDIENTS
    400g/14oz can condensed milk
    400g/14oz can evaporated
      (unsweetened condensed) milk

VARIATION
A classic trick to making low-maintenance *dulce de leche* is to cook a whole, closed can of condensed milk in a pan of boiling water for 30 minutes, but this must be done with care as the can could explode if not continuously immersed in water. South American cooks often add a can of condensed milk to the pan when cooking beans, so side dish and dessert cook together.

1 Combine the condensed and evaporated milk in a heavy pan. Place over a medium heat and bring to the boil. Reduce the heat slightly and cook, stirring constantly, for 30–35 minutes until thickened and toffee coloured. Use a relatively large pan, as the milk has a tendency to boil over.

2 Pour into a sterilized jar and seal. *Dulce de leche* will keep for months, but with time, the texture will alter and won't be as smooth.

3 Serve with ice cream, as a filling for pancakes or cakes, or even with a white cheese, such as ricotta.

BRAZILIAN COCONUT FLAN

THIS IS A SOMEWHAT UNCONVENTIONAL BUT VERY SUCCESSFUL RECIPE FOR QUINDAO, A CLASSIC BRAZILIAN DESSERT MADE WITH NO FEWER THAN 18 EGG YOLKS. IT IS AVAILABLE AS A PACKET MIX THROUGHOUT LATIN AMERICA, BUT IT IS MUCH MORE DELICIOUS IF YOU MAKE YOUR OWN.

SERVES TWELVE

INGREDIENTS
150g/5oz/1⅔ cups desiccated (dry unsweetened shredded) coconut
200ml/7fl oz/scant 1 cup full-fat (whole) milk
40g/1½oz/3 tbsp unsalted (sweet) butter, softened
400g/14oz/2 cups caster (superfine) sugar, plus extra for dusting
18 egg yolks

1 Put the desiccated coconut in a bowl. Pour over the milk and leave to stand for about 15 minutes, or until all the milk has been absorbed.

2 Meanwhile, grease a 23cm/9in ring mould with some of the butter and then lightly dust with a sprinkling of caster sugar.

3 Put the remaining butter in a large bowl. Add the sugar and soaked coconut, and mix vigorously until thoroughly combined.

4 Using a wooden spoon, gently stir in the egg yolks, one at a time. When the ingredients are thoroughly combined, cover the bowl with a clean dishtowel and leave the mixture to stand in a cool place for about 1 hour.

5 Tip the coconut mixture into the prepared ring mould and place this in the centre of a large, deep roasting pan. Pour in enough warm water to come halfway up the outside of the mould. Place this bain marie and its pudding in a cold oven.

6 Heat the oven to 220°C/425°F/Gas 7 and bake the flan for about 1 hour, or until the surface is a dark golden, caramelized brown. Remove from the oven and leave to cool in the water in the roasting pan.

7 When the flan is cold, loosen the edges carefully with a palette knife. Cover with an upturned serving platter and turn the ring mould gently upside down. Gently lift off the ring mould, being careful not to let it touch the top of the flan. Serve cut in thick slices.

VARIATIONS
When available, use finely grated fresh coconut instead of desiccated. There is no need to soak the fresh coconut in the milk; just add both ingredients to the butter and sugar. For a more fragrant, even sweeter flan, try adding a whole vanilla pod to the egg and coconut mixture before it is left to stand. Make sure you remove it before cooking.

NUTRITIONAL INFORMATION

The nutritional analysis below is per portion, unless otherwise stated.

p64 Corn Tortillas Energy 70Kcal/296kJ; Protein 0.1g; Carbohydrate 18.1g, of which sugars 0g; Fat 0.1g, of which saturates 0g; Cholesterol 0mg; Calcium 3mg; Fibre 0g; Sodium 10mg

p65 Flour Tortillas Energy 64Kcal/272kJ; Protein 1.5g; Carbohydrate 12.5g, of which sugars 0.2g; Fat 1.3g, of which saturates 0.5g; Cholesterol 1mg; Calcium 23mg; Fibre 0.5g; Sodium 140mg

p66 Corn Griddle Cakes Energy 87Kcal/366kJ; Protein 2.2g; Carbohydrate 12.5g, of which sugars 0.2g; Fat 3.5g, of which saturates 1.9g; Cholesterol 9mg; Calcium 50mg; Fibre 0g; Sodium 260mg

p68 Cassava Chips Energy 453Kcal/1900kJ; Protein 3g; Carbohydrate 56.4g, of which sugars 1.4g; Fat 25.6g, of which saturates 3.8g; Cholesterol 0mg; Calcium 30mg; Fibre 2.6g; Sodium 4mg

p69 Cheese Tamales Energy 197Kcal/825kJ; Protein 3.3g; Carbohydrate 21.2g, of which sugars 0.3g; Fat 11.6g, of which saturates 5.8g; Cholesterol 21mg; Calcium 80mg; Fibre 0.0g; Sodium 560mg

p70 Tamales de Picadillo Energy 188Kcal/785kJ; Protein 7.8g; Carbohydrate 14.7g, of which sugars 3.0g; Fat 11.3g, of which saturates 4.4g; Cholesterol 26mg; Calcium 13mg; Fibre 0.4g; Sodium 175mg

p71 Mixed Tostadas Energy 253Kcal/1068kJ; Protein 14.7g; Carbohydrate 32.8g, of which sugars 3.4g; Fat 7.9g, of which saturates 2.8g; Cholesterol 25mg; Calcium 192mg; Fibre 3.0g; Sodium 424mg

p72 Pan-fried Squid Energy 250Kcal/1043kJ; Protein 32.8g; Carbohydrate 2.6g, of which sugars 0.1g; Fat 9.2g, of which saturates 1.5g; Cholesterol 500mg; Calcium 33mg; Fibre 0g; Sodium 475mg

p72 Fried Whitebait with Cayenne Pepper Energy 328Kcal/1359kJ; Protein 12.2g; Carbohydrate 3.3g, of which sugars 0.1g; Fat 29.7g, of which saturates 5.9g; Cholesterol 0mg; Calcium 538mg; Fibre 0.1g; Sodium 144mg

p74 Black Eyed Bean and Shrimp Fritters Energy 136Kcal/570kJ; Protein 7.7g; Carbohydrate 14.7g, of which sugars 1.6g; Fat 5.5g, of which saturates 0.7g; Cholesterol 10mg; Calcium 33mg; Fibre 2.3g; Sodium 83mg

p75 Beef Empanadas Energy 138Kcal/579kJ; Protein 6.6g; Carbohydrate 12.7g, of which sugars 0.8g; Fat 7.1g, of which saturates 3.1g; Cholesterol 23mg; Calcium 20mg; Fibre 0.7g; Sodium 102mg

p76 Nut Brittle Energy 239Kcal/1005kJ; Protein 6.5g; Carbohydrate 29.3g, of which sugars 27.2g; Fat 11.5g, of which saturates 2.2g; Cholesterol 00mg; Calcium 22mg; Fibre 1.5g; Sodium 2mg

p76 Coconut Sweets Energy 40Kcal/168kJ; Protein 0.1g; Carbohydrate 7.4g, of which sugars 7.4g; Fat 1.2g, of which saturates 1.1g; Cholesterol 0mg; Calcium 3mg; Fibre 0.3g; Sodium 1mg

p80 Creamy Heart of Palm Soup Energy 441Kcal/1824kJ; Protein 4.9g; Carbohydrate 13.1g, of which sugars 7.1g; Fat 41.4g, of which saturates 24.5g; Cholesterol 99mg; Calcium 91mg; Fibre 4.5g; Sodium 219mg

p81 Peanut and Potato Soup with Coriander Energy 259Kcal/1076kJ; Protein 8.1g; Carbohydrate 14.5g, of which sugars 6.1g; Fat 19.2g, of which saturates 3.7g; Cholesterol 0mg; Calcium 30mg; Fibre 3.0g; Sodium 141mg

p82 Crab, Coconut and Coriander Soup Energy 232Kcal/972kJ; Protein 23.8g; Carbohydrate 7.4g, of which sugars 6.5g; Fat 12.2g, of which saturates 3.7g; Cholesterol 90mg; Calcium 188mg; Fibre 1.0g; Sodium 937mg

p83 Chilli Clam Broth Energy 141Kcal/595kJ; Protein 8.8g; Carbohydrate 11.0g, of which sugars 4.1g; Fat 4.3g,

of which saturates 0.7g; Cholesterol 31mg; Calcium 74mg; Fibre 1.2g; Sodium 403mg

p84 Chunky Prawn Chupe Energy 259Kcal/1089kJ; Protein 23.2g; Carbohydrate 26.8g, of which sugars 7.3g; Fat 7.3g, of which saturates 1.1g; Cholesterol 233mg; Calcium 125mg; Fibre 3.7g; Sodium 1.4g

p84 Corn Soup Energy 561Kcal/2330kJ; Protein 5.6g; Carbohydrate 39.2g, of which sugars 16.3g; Fat 43.6g, of which saturates 26.3g; Cholesterol 107mg; Calcium 54mg; Fibre 2.6g; Sodium 577mg

p88 Baked Sea Bass with Coconut Energy 227Kcal/961kJ; Protein 38.2g; Carbohydrate 5.4g, of which sugars 4.6g; Fat 6.1g, of which saturates 0.9g; Cholesterol 95mg; Calcium 125mg; Fibre 0.5g; Sodium 326mg

p88 Pan-Fried Sea Bream with Lime and Tomato Salsa Energy 208Kcal/870kJ; Protein 28.1g; Carbohydrate 2.5g, of which sugars 2.5g; Fat 9.5g, of which saturates 1.4g; Cholesterol 69mg; Calcium 21mg; Fibre 0.8g; Sodium 97mg

p90 Halibut with Peppers and Coconut Milk Energy 279Kcal/1175kJ; Protein 23.8g; Carbohydrate 19.9g, of which sugars 7.5g; Fat 12.3g, of which saturates 5.6g; Cholesterol 41mg; Calcium 48mg; Fibre 2.3g; Sodium 122mg

p91 Prawn and Potato Omelette Energy 195Kcal/814kJ; Protein 16.0g; Carbohydrate 9.0g, of which sugars 3.4g; Fat 10.8g, of which saturates 2.5g; Cholesterol 320mg; Calcium 85mg; Fibre 1.2g; Sodium 659mg

p92 Sea Bass Ceviche Energy 183Kcal/776kJ; Protein 30.6g; Carbohydrate 9.7g, of which sugars 8.9g; Fat 2.8g, of which saturates 0.4g; Cholesterol 101mg; Calcium 51mg; Fibre 1.0g; Sodium 171mg

p93 Mackerel Escabeche Energy 576Kcal/2393kJ; Protein 38.5g; Carbohydrate 8.4g, of which sugars 1.5g; Fat 43.3g, of which saturates 8.2g; Cholesterol 108mg; Calcium 40mg; Fibre 0.6g; Sodium 127mg

p94 Marinated Red Mullet Energy 338Kcal/1408kJ; Protein 29.9g; Carbohydrate 12.3g, of which sugars 7.2g; Fat 19.1g, of which saturates

2.8g; Cholesterol 69mg; Calcium 60mg; Fibre 3.9g; Sodium 636mg

p95 Cod Caramba Energy 307Kcal/1286kJ; Protein 20.6g; Carbohydrate 18.5g, of which sugars 7.1g; Fat 14.1g, of which saturates 6.9g; Cholesterol 78mg; Calcium 119mg; Fibre 2.7g; Sodium 720mg

p96 King Prawns in a Coconut and Nut Cream Energy 496Kcal/2072kj; Protein 46.5g; Carbohydrate 18.1g, of which sugars 6.4g; Fat 26.8g, of which saturates 12.5g; Cholesterol 448mg; Calcium 254mg; Fibre 2.3g; Sodium 2.8g

p97 Stuffed Crab Energy 162 Kcal/680kj; Protein 15.9g; Carbohydrate 8.7g, of which sugars 3.5g; Fat 7.3g, of which saturates3.7g; Cholesterol 129mg; Calcium 162mg; Fibre 0.9g; Sodium 475mg

p98 Chilean Squid Casserole Energy 260Kcal/1089kJ; Protein 19.9g; Carbohydrate 17.2g, of which sugars 3.5g; Fat 8.1g, of which saturates 1.3g; Cholesterol 267mg; Calcium 42mg; Fibre 1.5g; Sodium 333mg

p99 Chilean Seafood Platter Energy 205Kcal/863kJ; Protein 32.7g; Carbohydrate 3.5g, of which sugars 0.5g; Fat 6.8g, of which saturates 1.1g; Cholesterol 267mg; Calcium 146mg; Fibre 0.4g; Sodium 1.6g

p102 The Gaucho Barbecue Energy 839Kcal/3501kJ; Protein 88.1g; Carbohydrate 3.8g, of which sugars 1.1g; Fat 52.5g, of which saturates 22.5g; Cholesterol 249mg; Calcium 63mg; Fibre 0.4g; Sodium 1.2g

p103 Beef Stuffed with Eggs and Spinach Energy 318Kcal/1328kJ; Protein 39.0g; Carbohydrate 3.4g, of which sugars 2.8g; Fat 16.7g, of which saturates 4.6g; Cholesterol 161mg; Calcium 103mg; Fibre 1.6g; Sodium 299mg

p104 Feijoada Energy 779Kcal/3262kJ; Protein 58.0g; Carbohydrate 49.9g, of which sugars 3.8g; Fat 39.9g, of which saturates 13.5g; Cholesterol 142mg; Calcium 135mg; Fibre 7.3g; Sodium 1.5g

p106 Black Bean Chilli con Carne Energy 374Kcal/1575kJ; Protein 39.0g; Carbohydrate 27.9g, of which sugars 7.4g; Fat 12.6g, of which saturates 4.1g; Cholesterol 83mg; Calcium 60mg; Fibre 4.7g; Sodium 111mg

p107 Mexican Spicy Beef Tortilla
Energy 595Kcal/2516kJ; Protein 30.3g;
Carbohydrate 91.2g, of which sugars
11.5g; Fat 14.7g, of which saturates
4.7g; Cholesterol 53mg; Calcium
153mg; Fibre 4.0g; Sodium 379mg

**p108 Spicy Meatballs with Tomato
Sauce** Energy 552Kcal/2296kJ; Protein
29.9g; Carbohydrate 21.8g, of which
sugars 6.0g; Fat 39.0g, of which saturates
11.6g; Cholesterol 132mg; Calcium
75mg; Fibre 2.0g; Sodium 268mg

p109 Scrambled Eggs with Chorizo
Energy 322Kcal/1335kJ; Protein 20.3g;
Carbohydrate 5.7g, of which sugars
0.6g; Fat 24.3g, of which saturates
7.6g; Cholesterol 472mg; Calcium
101mg; Fibre 0.3g; Sodium 687mg

p110 Spiced Roast Leg of Lamb Energy
470Kcal/1962kJ; Protein 37.2g;
Carbohydrate 22.6g, of which sugars
6.5g; Fat 24.9g, of which saturates
9.1g; Cholesterol 117mg; Calcium
38mg; Fibre 7.4g; Sodium 651mg

p111 Rabbit in Coconut Milk Energy
301Kcal/1260kJ; Protein 29.9g;
Carbohydrate 10.8g, of which sugars
9.2g; Fat 15.7g, of which saturates
4.0g; Cholesterol 68mg; Calcium 73mg;
Fibre 1.5g; Sodium 236mg

**p112 Pork Roasted with Herbs, Spices
and Rum** Energy 410Kcal/1712kJ;
Protein 42.4g; Carbohydrate 3.9g,
of which sugars 3.8g; Fat 21.4g, of
which saturates 8.2g; Cholesterol
132mg; Calcium 16mg; Fibre 0.1g;
Sodium 577mg

p113 Pork with Pineapple Energy
492Kcal/2041kJ; Protein 28.7g;
Carbohydrate 12.9g, of which sugars
12.2g; Fat 36.4g, of which saturates
12.6g; Cholesterol 92mg; Calcium 30mg;
Fibre 1.2g; Sodium 136g

p114 Carbonada Criolla Energy 505Kcal/
2124kJ; Protein 46.1g; Carbohydrate
33.6g, of which sugars 11.4g; Fat 18.3g,
of which saturates 6.1g; Cholesterol
125mg; Calcium 44mg; Fibre 3.6g;
Sodium 175mg

p118 Cuban Chicken Pie Energy
521Kcal/2814kJ; Protein 39.8g;
Carbohydrate 35.2g, of which sugars
20.1g; Fat 25.6g, of which saturates
10.8g; Cholesterol 324g; Calcium
62mg; Fibre 2.5g; Sodium 0.19g

p119 Chicken with Okra Energy
122Kcal/511kJ; Protein 10.8g;
Carbohydrate 9.7g, of which sugars

7.9g; Fat 4.8g, of which saturates 1.0g;
Cholesterol 32g; Calcium 162mg;
Fibre 5.1g; Sodium 0.04g

p120 Colombian Chicken Hot-pot Energy
368Kcal/1559kJ; Protein 29.2g;
Carbohydrate 49.6g, of which sugars
6.5g; Fat 7.2g, of which saturates 1.8g;
Cholesterol 107; Calcium 29mg;
Fibre 3.7g; Sodium 0.19g

**p122 Chicken, Pork and Potatoes in
Peanut Sauce** Energy 405Kcal/1697kJ;
Protein 41.1g; Carbohydrate 18.2g, of
which sugars 4.1g; Fat 19.0g, of
which saturates 3.8g; Cholesterol
105g; Calcium 40mg; Fibre 2.5g;
Sodium 0.44g

p124 Peruvian Duck with Rice Energy
527Kcal/2207kJ; Protein 17.6g;
Carbohydrate 55.2g, of which sugars
2.8g; Fat 24.6g, of which saturates
7.2g; Cholesterol 58mg; Calcium 62mg;
Fibre 1.8g; Sodium 100mg

p124 Drunken Duck Energy 693Kcal/
2895kJ; Protein 24.7g; Carbohydrate
45.5g, of which sugars 14.9g; Fat
41.7g, of which saturates 12.5g;
Cholesterol 106mg; Calcium 91mg;
Fibre 5.6g; Sodium 220mg

p128 Corn Soufflé Energy 385Kcal/
1605kJ; Protein 15.2g; Carbohydrate
25.3g, of which sugars 8.7g; Fat 25.5g,
of which saturates 13.7g; Cholesterol
246mg; Calcium 246mg; Fibre 2.5g;
Sodium 480mg

p129 Layered Potato Bake with Cheese
Energy 442Kcal/1831kJ; Protein 12.2g;
Carbohydrate 16.3g, of which sugars
4.1g; Fat 36.9g, of which saturates
7.2g; Cholesterol 132mg; Calcium
137mg; Fibre 2.4g; Sodium 610mg

p130 Heart of Palm Pie Energy
566Kcal/2361kJ; Protein 10.8g;
Carbohydrate 57.1g, of which sugars
6.3g; Fat 34.2g, of which saturates
18.2g; Cholesterol 139mg; Calcium
164mg; Fibre 4.4g; Sodium 430,g

p132 Avocado and Grapefruit Salad
Energy 351Kcal/1448kJ; Protein 2.5g;
Carbohydrate 5.4g, of which sugars
4.0g; Fat 35.7g, of which saturates
6.4g; Cholesterol 0mg; Calcium 28mg;
Fibre 4.1g; Sodium 80mg

p133 Quinoa Salad with Citrus Dressing
Energy 225Kcal/938kJ; Protein 4.1g;
Carbohydrate 22.1g, of which sugars
3.1g; Fat 13.9g, of which saturates
2.1g; Cholesterol 0mg; Calcium 40mg;
Fibre 3.0g; Sodium 10mg

p134 Okra and Tomato Salad Energy
154Kcal/639kJ; Protein 3.7g;
Carbohydrate 7.9g, of which sugars
6.6g; Fat 12.3g, of which saturates 1.9g;
Cholesterol 0mg; Calcium 174mg;
Fibre 5.2g; Sodium 15mg

**p134 Tomato, Heart of Palm and Onion
Salad** Energy 152Kcal/632kJ; Protein
2.8g; Carbohydrate 8.7g, of which
sugars 7.7g; Fat 12.0g, of which
saturates 1.8g; Cholesterol 0mg;
Calcium 38mg; Fibre 3.9g; Sodium 16mg

p136 Peruvian Salad Energy 226Kcal/
945kJ; Protein 6.2g; Carbohydrate
23.1g, of which sugars 4.6g; Fat 12.7g,
of which saturates 2.6g; Cholesterol
78mg; Calcium 59mg; Fibre 3.3g;
Sodium 570mg

p137 Pumpkin Salad Energy 384Kcal/
1583kJ; Protein 2.2g; Carbohydrate
8.7g, of which sugars 6.5g; Fat
38.1g, of which saturates 5.5g;
Cholesterol 0mg; Calcium 84mg;
Fibre 3.0g; Sodium 10mg

140 Plain Rice Energy 241Kcal/
1018kJ; Protein 3.7g; Carbohydrate
42.9g, of which sugars 0g; Fat 7.3g,
of which saturates 1.1g; Cholesterol
0mg; Calcium 26mg; Fibre 0.2g;
Sodium 0mg

p140 Black Beans Energy 319Kcal/
1347kJ; Protein 20.7g; Carbohydrate
40.6g, of which sugars 2.2g; Fat 9.4g,
of which saturates 2.4g; Cholesterol
12mg; Calcium 62mg; Fibre 6.2g;
Sodium 250mg

p142 Cassava with a Citrus Salsa Energy
305Kcal/1294kJ; Protein 3g;
Carbohydrate 57.2g, of which sugars
2.2g; Fat 8.9g, of which saturates 1.4g;
Cholesterol 0mg; Calcium 31mg; Fibre
2.6g; Sodium 0mg

p143 Stir-Fried Spring Greens Energy
111Kcal/459kJ; Protein 6.3g;
Carbohydrate 2.5g, of which sugars 2g;
Fat 8.5g, of which saturates 2.3g;
Cholesterol 16mg; Calcium 159mg;
Fibre 2.6g; Sodium 330mg

p144 Argentinian Barbecue Salsa
Energy 132Kcal/543kJ; Protein 0.7g;
Carbohydrate 3.2g, of which sugars
2.6g; Fat 13g, of which saturates 1.9g;
Cholesterol 0mg; Calcium 10mg; Fibre
0.8g; Sodium 0mg

p144 Hot Chilli Salsa Energy 441Kcal/
1820kJ; Protein 3.8g; Carbohydrate
5.8g, of which sugars 5.8g; Fat 45g, of
which saturates 6.4g; Cholesterol 0mg;
Calcium 40mg; Fibre 1.5g; Sodium 20mg

p146 Tamarillo Sauce Energy 112Kcal/
468kJ; Protein 0.7g; Carbohydrate
15.5g, of which sugars 15.2g; Fat 5.7g,
of which saturates 0.8g; Cholesterol
0mg; Calcium 9mg; Fibre 2.2g;
Sodium 0mg

p147 Avocado Salsa Energy 190Kcal/
786kJ; Protein 1.9g; Carbohydrate 5.6g,
of which sugars 4g; Fat 18g, of which
saturates 3.2g; Cholesterol 0mg;
Calcium 20mg; Fibre 3g; Sodium 10mg

p150 Mango Sorbet Energy 176Kcal/
753kJ; Protein 1g; Carbohydrate
45.6g, of which sugars 45.4g;
Fat 0.2g, of which saturates 0.1g;
Cholesterol 0mg; Calcium 13mg;
Fibre 2g; Sodium 10mg

p151 Colombian Pineapple Custard
Energy 214Kcal/908kJ; Protein 5.3g;
Carbohydrate 40.5g, of which sugars
40.5g; Fat 4.6g, of which saturates
1.3g; Cholesterol 156mg; Calcium
38mg; Fibre 0.7g; Sodium 60mg

p152 Coconut and Pumpkin Compote
Energy 429Kcal/1811kJ; Protein 2g;
Carbohydrate 82.9g, of which sugars
82.2g; Fat 12.2g, of which saturates
10.4g; Cholesterol 0mg; Calcium 51mg;
Fibre 4g; Sodium 100mg

p152 Dulce de Leche Energy 323Kcal/
1357kJ; Protein 11.3g; Carbohydrate
42.7g, of which sugars 42.7g; Fat
13g, of which saturates 8.1g;
Cholesterol 47mg; Calcium 387mg;
Fibre 0g; Sodium 210mg

p154 Brazilian Coconut Flan Energy
334Kcal/1398kJ; Protein 5.6g;
Carbohydrate 36.6g, of which sugars
36.6g; Fat 19.4g, of which saturates
11.2g; Cholesterol 312mg; Calcium
62mg; Fibre 1.7g; Sodium 50mg

INDEX